BATHROOMS

How to

Real People – Real Projects™

HOMETIME®

Publisher: Dean Johnson
Editor: Pamela S. Price
Writer: James A. Hufnagel
Art Director: Bill Nelson
Copy Editor: Lisa Wagner

Hometime Hosts: Dean Johnson, Robin Hartl
Project Producer: Matt Dolph
Construction and Technical Review: Dean Doying,
Mark Kimball, Dan Laabs

Illustrator: Mario Ferro
Photographer: Jeff Lyman
Cover Photo: Maki Strunc Photography
Location Photography Manager: Michael Klaers
Studio Photography Manager: Jason Adair
Video Frame Capture: Julie Wallace

Production Coordinator: Pam Scheunemann
Electronic Layout: Chris Long

Book Creative Direction, Design, and Production:
MacLean & Tuminelly, Minneapolis, MN
Cover Design: Richard Scales Advertising Associates

Library of Congress Catalog Card Number 96-80445
ISBN 1-890257-00-1

HOMETIME®
4275 Norex Drive
Chaska, MN 55318

Special Thanks: Bob Dempsey, Congoleum
Corporation; Bill Erbstoesser, Kohler; Terry
Fitzpatrick, Mannington Resilent Floors; Kate
Hilgenberg, Jerry's Floor Store; Bill Hoffman,
NIOSH; Jack McCarthy, McCarthy Plumbing; Mary Jo
Peterson CKD, CBD; Joann Weeden, American
Standard; Scott Wise, Armstrong World Industries

Contributing Photography: American Shower &
Bath/Trayco, American Woodmark, Angelo
Lighting, Ann Sacks Tile & Stone, Armstrong World
Industries, Avonite, Broan Mfg. Co., Cold Spring
Granite, Congoleum, Country Floors, DuPont Nylon
Furnishings, Finnleo/Saunatec, Florida Tile, Kohler
Company, Lippert Corporation, Merillat Industries,
Myson, Sloan Flushmate, Wilsonart

5 4 3 2 1   02 01 00 99 98

Electronic Prepress: Encore Color Group
Printed by: Quebecor Printing

Printed in the United States

*For online project help and information on other
Hometime products, visit us on the Web at*
www.hometime.com

Introduction

We've often said that one of the main advantages to doing your own home improvements is that you can plow the whole budget into materials and design, ending up with a better-looking result than if you spent the same amount to hire the job done. Never is this more true than when remodeling a bathroom. For the money you would pay to have someone else provide the labor, you can afford to upgrade the quality of the products you install – from the flooring to the fixtures.

Unfortunately, the job tends to take longer when you do it yourself since you can usually only chip away at it evenings and weekends. This will wreak havoc with your daily schedule, especially if your house has only one bathroom. A bathroom's true purpose may be utilitarian, but we've all become accustomed to a certain degree of comfort in this room. Making do with cat-baths at the kitchen sink for a week or two is going to test the patience of any family. Thorough planning is the key to an efficient remodel with minimal inconvenience.

Work safely and, when you're all done, go treat yourself to some soft new bath towels and enjoy that hot steamy shower in your new bathroom – you earned it.

Table of Contents

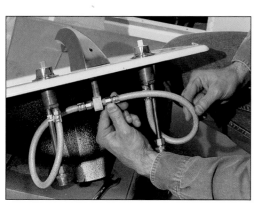

PLANNING and PREPARATION

Any successful remodel *starts with a plan. A carefully thought-out plan sets out critical specifications for any contractors you hire, and serves as a key document in your application for a building permit.*

Thinking through a bathroom project calls for some other paperwork, too. Now, before you pick up any tool heavier than a tape measure, is the time to establish a budget, analyze the situation at your house, nail down costs, and resolve structural issues. You also need to decide how much of the work you realistically can do yourself and create a schedule that will keep the project flowing smoothly.

Budget

How much will it cost to remodel your bathroom or to add a new one? The answer depends on how much you're willing and able to spend. As with any remodeling project, the biggest potential for savings is in your own hands – doing the work yourself can pare your budget by about 50 percent.

What's typical?

You might be surprised to learn that many bathroom remodels cost less than $5,000, and some come in under $2,000. With that kind of a budget, you can replace a fixture or two, tile the walls (and maybe the floor), and add or upgrade amenities such as the vanity, medicine cabinet, lighting, and ventilation. Of course, doing all or most of the work yourself makes more of your budget available for new materials or better-quality fixtures.

To help keep the budget down, ask yourself if you really need to replace all of the fixtures, especially the tub. Often, all that's needed to give an old, worn tub a like-new look is a professional resurfacing. A bathroom sink also can be resurfaced, and then updated with a new faucet.

If you're adding a brand new bathroom, you can expect to pay at least a few thousand dollars more for additional plumbing, structural work, and fixtures.

What's it worth?

While the cash you put into improvements seldom yields a dollar-for-dollar return at resale, bathrooms score high among typical upgrades – with a 60 to 80 percent return for a remodel, and a 75 to 100 percent return for a new second bathroom.

Keep in mind, though, that local market conditions will influence the resale value of any improvements. If you're planning to sell in the next few years, ask a real estate agent for comparables to help determine what size budget makes sense for your neighborhood.

Finally, realize that the real payback for any remodel is what it's worth to you. You'll enjoy a new bathroom day in and day out for years to come, and that's often reason enough for making the investment.

Budget busters

Extensive plumbing and structural work can add thousands of dollars to the bill. Replacing old fixtures with new ones is usually fairly simple, but moving fixtures (especially a toilet) means you might need a plumber to run new pipes.

In the bathroom shown here, moving the toilet entailed opening up a ceiling and wall below and installing a new soil stack and drain pipes.

Get prices for each and every element that will go into your bathroom project. Make lists that include model numbers, colors, and other vital information. As you research prices for fixtures and materials, compile two lists – one for items you wish you could have and another for those you realistically can afford. You might find that by juggling the budget at least a few of your wishes make the final lineup.

Rainy day fund

After you've done all your homework and determined how much you can afford to spend on your bathroom project, reduce the budget by 10 to 20 percent. Put this money in a contingency fund to cover unexpected costs.

Even the best-planned projects yield surprises. You might discover that pipes and wires aren't always exactly where you think they should be, or that the subflooring under the toilet needs to be replaced. Even nickel-and-dime surprises can add up to a lot of money. A contingency fund covers these expenses and assures you won't have to scramble for more funding to finish your project.

Avoid change orders

If you're hiring a contractor, it pays to finalize your plan before work begins. You want to keep change orders to a minimum – any work not specified in the original contract will cost extra and can quickly destroy a budget.

Avoid the phrase "while you're at it" at all costs. It's far too easy to get caught up in a remodeling fever and expand far beyond the original scope of the project. Remember that every time you say "while you're at it" to a contractor, you create a change order that will drive up the cost of your job.

Don't go overboard *remodeling a family or guest bathroom. New faucets, a fiberglass tub surround, and a refinished tub will set you back around $500.*

A big-budget bathroom remodel *often features high-end fixtures, such as this luxurious shower. It features both a traditional showerhead and a multi-head, full-body spray. Cost: $3,000–$3,250.*

What will it cost?

Item	Standard	Deluxe	Super deluxe
Toilets	$90–140	$200–300	$700–1,600
Sinks	$50–125	$250–300	$500–600
Bathtubs	$100–200	$300–400	$600–800
Sink faucet	$80	$125	$500
Shower/tub faucet	$100	$250	$500
Vanity cabinet (24x18")	$80–100	$200	$350
Linen cabinet (84" high, width varies)	$130	$350	$1,000
Medicine cabinet	$50–100	$200	$500
Vanity light	$50	$100	$300
Fan/light combo	$50	$130	$400
Ceramic tile (sq. ft.)			
4x4"	$1–2	$3–4	$5+
8x8"	$1–3	$3–4	$10+
12x12"	$2–3	$5–6	$10+
Vinyl flooring (sq. ft.)	$1	$3	$8–12

Assess Your Needs

You're probably all too familiar with the shortcomings of your present bathroom, but it's still a good idea to write them down and list possible solutions alongside the problems. Stay flexible at this point. There's usually more than one answer, and the first idea that occurs to you might not be the best.

What's wrong?

Most older bathrooms suffer at least one, or even all of these ills.

- Too small? Consider expanding into an adjacent closet or hallway, or even part of a bedroom.
- Awkward layout? Older bathrooms often suffer from chronic layout problems: a long, narrow plan that wastes floor space, for example, or a door that bangs into a fixture every time it's opened. Relocating a fixture or moving a wall might make a big difference.
- Short on storage? Consider a bigger vanity and larger medicine cabinet. See if the space can be reconfigured so there's room

After. An adjacent dressing room was annexed to double the size of this master bathroom. Ceramic tile wainscoting, a marble floor, and new fixtures complete the transformation.

Before. With fixtures crammed together, the old bathroom begged for more elbow room. Both the toilet and the sink had seen better days.

Before. Lack of storage space drove previous owners to create a crude medicine cabinet in dead space between wall studs.

for a linen closet or cabinet.

- Worn and/or dated fixtures and materials? How are the tub and sink surfaces holding up? Is your bathroom cursed with a funky color scheme from several decades ago? New tile, flooring, and fixtures can change all that.
- Poor lighting? If you can't get a good, shadow-free look at yourself, include new lighting fixtures in your plan.
- Poor ventilation? If the walls break into a sweat every time someone showers, budget for a power ventilator.

Who will use the bathroom?

Are you remodeling a family bathroom, a master suite bathroom, or a guest bathroom? Each has slightly different requirements.

A family bathroom should allow two people to comfortably share the space. Dual sinks and a wall and door separating the sink from the tub and toilet will cut down on congestion during the morning rush hour.

A master suite bathroom could benefit from a more open scheme, with less division between bathing and sleeping areas. Consider going upscale with a master bathroom, and include fixtures such as a whirlpool tub and/or a separate shower. You'll recoup some of your investment when you sell, and in the meantime, you'll enjoy the amenities.

Remodeling a guest bathroom or powder room usually provides the least return, so don't go overboard here. A new sink and faucet, color scheme, towels, and accessories might be all you need to help visitors feel more at home.

After. A few more feet of space, new cabinets, sink, flooring, and lighting transformed the bathroom shown below into a welcoming space.

Before. Years of caustic drain cleaners destroyed the finish on this cast-iron tub. The faucet and plastic tub surround were also due for replacement.

Before. A single medicine cabinet and a wall-hung sink didn't even come close to providing storage for all the stuff that accumulates in today's bathrooms.

The luxury of a home spa

Just about any amenity you've enjoyed at a health club can be installed for home use. Special equipment converts an ordinary stall shower into a steam bath. Saunas are available in ready-to-assemble kits or site-built, custom designs. Saunas range from a cozy fit for two to accommodations to seat the whole family. If you have the space, take the spa concept a step further and install home exercise equipment in the bathroom or an adjoining room.

What is Universal Design?

Universal design (also known as barrier-free design or just UD) provides guidelines for creating space that can be easily used by anyone. This includes people who are short, tall, young, old, in wheelchairs, or have limited range of motion.

Incorporating universal design

Universal design specifications go well beyond what most building codes require. For instance, to accommodate wheelchair users, UD calls for doorways that are at least 32 inches wide, as opposed to the standard 28-inch width. Toilets need to be 18 inches high or equipped with a special seat that adds 3 inches to the standard 15-inch height. Grab bars and 2 to 3 feet of clear space to the front and side of a toilet make it easier to transfer from a wheelchair.

In addition to providing space for wheelchairs, UD guidelines make a bathroom safer and more comfortable for everyone. Paddle handles, for example, make operating faucets more convenient, and pressure-balancing valves (also called anti-scald valves) prevent serious burns, a particular problem for elderly people and for young children. An adjustable-height showerhead makes showering more pleasant for people of all heights, whether they are seated or standing. Countertops in a color that contrasts with the floor color, or with a contrasting-color edge band, make it easier for people with failing sight to see the edge of the countertop. Tub and shower controls offset to the room-side of the tub mean you don't have to lean over so far (and risk losing your balance) when turning on the water, plus it's quicker for another person to turn off water in case of an emergency.

Best of all, accessibility doesn't have to look institutional. Many elements of UD can be accomplished using standard products and materials. Specialty items, such as grab bars, are now available in a variety of styles and colors.

Is UD for you?

Unless you're adding an entirely new bathroom, you probably can't make your bathroom totally barrier-free. But because universal design features make life smoother for everyone, it's worth incorporating them if you can. While walls are open, for example, it costs next to nothing to install blocking for future grab bars in the shower and next to the toilet. If you're moving a door, consider adding a couple inches to its width.

Need more information?

Universal design covers much more than bathrooms. There isn't a room in the house that can't be modified to create a barrier-free environment. There are even design guidelines for garages.

For more information about universal design, contact:
Center for Universal Design
(800/647-6777)
National Kitchen and Bath Association
(800/843-6522, ask for the UD guidelines)
U.S. Access Board
(800/872-2253)

In this barrier-free bathroom the shower is large enough to accommodate a wheelchair and it has a pan with a ramp edge so a chair can roll in easily. Faucets are within easy reach of a seated person.

A wall-hung sink lets a wheelchair-user fit his or her knees underneath. The sink's pipes are covered to prevent burns.

A clear floor space 60 inches in diameter provides room to turn a wheelchair.

Structural Issues

Before you put pencil to paper, bear in mind that certain aspects of your present bathroom will be difficult, expensive, or even impossible to change. Here's a brief rundown.

- Stealing space. You can usually expand a bathroom into an adjacent closet or bedroom, but building codes don't allow hallways that are less than 36 to 40 inches wide.
- Moving fixtures. With only minor plumbing changes you can relocate a sink or tub a few feet in one direction or the other, but plan to leave a toilet where it is if you can. Moving a toilet is an expensive job that calls for a professional plumber.
- Mechanical upgrades. If you have your heart set on an oversize tub, you may need a bigger water heater to supply it. And if you're adding a bathroom, will you need to extend new heating and cooling ducts?
- Mandated upgrades. Many codes specify that if you open a wall, all exposed wiring must be brought up to code, whether it was part of your original plan or not. You may also be required to install hard-wired smoke detectors.

Before. *Opening the wall uncovered this typical sink hookup. Small-diameter pipes bring water to shutoff valves; a rag plugs the opening where the trap empties into a drain pipe.*

After. *New copper pipes extend the water supply lines to the new sink location; plastic pipe does the same for the drain line. Be sure to check local codes before you decide to move a fixture.*

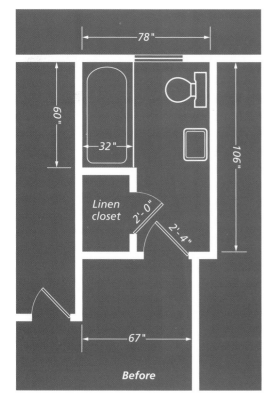

Before

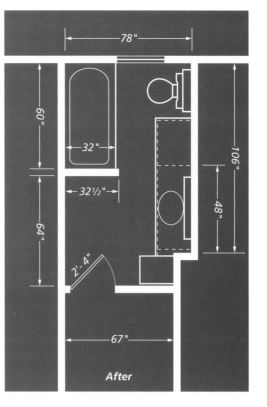

After

Can you steal some extra space?

The bathroom shown in the *before* plan originally included a big linen closet that wasted space and had a door that collided with the main door.

As seen in the *after* plan, removing the closet and bumping one wall a couple feet into the hallway freed up bathroom floor space. A new linen cabinet to the right of the relocated door replaces the old closet.

Architectural Symbols

Use these symbols to clarify a plan for yourself and others.

Plans

You've set a budget, identified the problems you want to solve, and wish-listed the amenities you'd like to have. Now it's time to get your new bathroom down on paper. Creating an accurate, to-scale plan is a dry run of the work ahead. It also will be a key page in your application for a building permit and in agreements with any contractors you decide to hire.

Do you need a designer?

If your ideas call for extensive plumbing work or you have a lot of unanswered questions, the answer is a definite maybe. A professional designer – look for one certified by the National Kitchen and Bath Association (NKBA) – can suggest different layout options and also draft your final working plan.

Design help may be as near as your favorite home center. Many kitchen and bathroom departments offer NKBA-certified designers working with computerized design programs to help you explore all your options. After you've settled on a plan, the computer prints out your working drawing which often includes a comprehensive shopping list of the materials your design will require.

Make a rough sketch

Regardless of who designs your bathroom, the process begins with a sketch of the space as it is now. Don't worry about straight lines and exact dimensions at this point; just be sure to draw in every nook and cranny.

Next, walk around the room, measuring every element with a tape measure. Double-check each measurement and note it on your sketch. Include the widths of door and window openings (including trim) and the distances between them. Also indicate the distances between fixtures and arcs for door swings.

Measure the room *with a steel tape rule. (Don't use cloth, it stretches.) Note all dimensions first on a rough sketch, then incorporate them into a scale plan.*

How to use architects' tools

A handful of tools and supplies, available at art and drafting supply stores, make drawing plans much easier.

- An architects' rule, marked in differing increments per foot, saves counting the squares on the graph paper when you're drawing up a room.
- A template makes it easier to sketch fixtures and other standard components. Stores typically stock ¼-inch scale templates; a ½-inch scale template will probably have to be special-ordered.

- A clear plastic triangle works better than a ruler for drawing lines that are perfectly straight and at exact 90- and 45-degree angles to each other.
- Graph paper, gridded with ¼- and ½-inch squares, helps you draw to scale. Use it in combination with an architect's rule.
- Tracing paper and drafting vellum are semi-transparent. Tape either over a graph paper outline of the space and draw in the different layouts you're considering.
- A mechanical architect's pencil is nice but not necessary; it saves sharpening and resharpening an ordinary pencil.

Draw a scale plan

Now transfer the information on your sketch to ¼-inch or ½-inch graph paper. While ¼-inch scale (¼ inch = 1 foot) is the standard architectural scale, we sometimes like to use ½-inch scale to draw a bathroom. You'll still be able to fit most bathrooms on one sheet of graph paper, and the larger scale makes it easier to draw and read the plan.

Take your time and double-check all dimensions. To account for the thickness of walls, represent them with a pair of lines. Even though your plan has been drawn to scale, you still need to write down all the critical dimensions.

Once you have an accurate drawing of your present bathroom, tape tracing paper over it and sketch the space the way you'd like it to be. Pay special attention to the fixture clearances and other typical dimensions shown below. If you don't like what you see, tear off the tracing paper and start with a fresh sheet.

Finally, when everything's laid out the way you want it, refer to the tracing paper and make an accurate, detailed plan of the way your bathroom will look after remodeling.

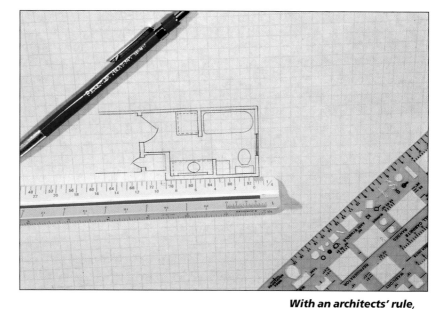

With an architects' rule, *template, graph paper, and a good, sharp pencil, you can create a professional-looking plan.*

Again, double-check all dimensions and indicate critical measurements in inches or in feet and inches. Note the scale you're using, and be sure your name and address are on the plan. Make photocopies for your permit application and for each contractor you'll be asking to bid on the job.

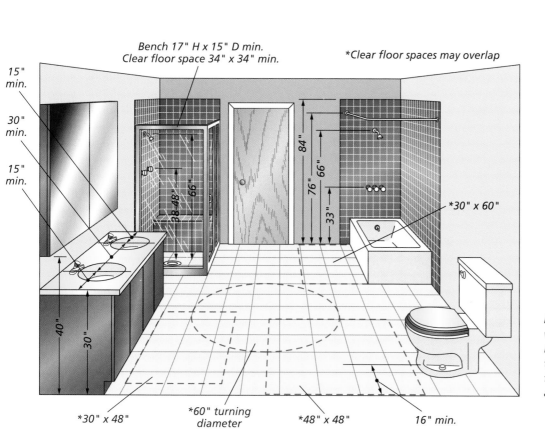

Bench 17" H x 15" D min.
Clear floor space 34" x 34" min.

*Clear floor spaces may overlap

15" min.

30" min.

15" min.

84"

76" 66"

33"

38"-48" 66"

*30" x 60"

40"

30"

*30" x 48"

*60" turning diameter

*48" x 48"

16" min.

Refer to these dimensions *when you're planning a new bathroom. A 60-inch-diameter space is recommended for turning a wheelchair around.*

How Much Can You Do Yourself?

Clearly, part of the answer to this question depends on how much you're willing to take on. But codes in your community also may rule out certain jobs you're not even allowed to do yourself. Chief among these are plumbing and wiring work, which may be off-limits to anyone but a licensed tradesman. Check with your building department to find out which jobs a homeowner can tackle in your town.

Any work, whether done by the homeowner or a contractor, must meet local building codes. Codes can vary widely from community to community, so make it your business to find out what's required in your area – before you start the project. Local building departments, and many public libraries, have copies of the code you can look at.

General contractors

A general contractor (often called a general or a GC) oversees a project from start to finish. A GC pulls the permits, lines up and supervises subcontractors, orders materials, schedules the work, arranges inspections, hauls away debris, and takes on all the headaches. He or she also marks up the cost of labor and materials, making a GC the most expensive way to go.

Do you really need a GC? For a straightforward bathroom remodel, probably not. With

How long can you live like this? You don't need a lot of specialized skills to gut an old bathroom and build a new one – but the project can easily drag out over a month or more of evenings and weekends.

a little organization you can handle the paperwork yourself, do all or most of the work, and hire subcontractors for the rest.

Subcontractors

Subcontractors (subs for short) specialize in one particular trade. The two subs you'll most likely use, plumbers and electricians, must be licensed to do work in your community. A license ensures that the sub understands and adheres to local building codes; a plumber

Get bids from at least three subcontractors for any parts of the job you plan to hire out. Request written bids with itemized breakdowns for labor and materials; this lets you know each bidder understands the full scope of the job.

or electrician who violates codes could lose his or her license. (Licenses aren't required for most other trades, though GCs are licensed in some states.)

Shop for a sub as you would for any other professional. Check with friends and co-workers who have recently had work done. Besides having a license, any sub you consider should also be bonded, insured against property damage, and have workers compensation coverage.

As you check out candidates, find out how long each has been in business. Ask for references and talk with homeowners they've done work for. After you've narrowed the field to three subs, it's time to ask for bids.

Bids

The key to getting bids is to make sure all potential subs are bidding on exactly the same job. Invite each one to drop by your home and look over the situation, then sit down and go over your plan. Be clear about who will supply fixtures and other materials, and who will arrange for permits and inspections. Discuss a time frame, too. Determine how long will it take to do the work, and when the sub will be available.

After the bids come in, analyze them carefully. Be suspicious of one that's substantially lower than the others. The bidder may be missing something or intending to cut corners, and is likely to ask for more money later. A high bid could mean that the contractor is already very busy and not interested in the job unless it pays better than the going rate.

Contracts

After choosing a contractor or subcontractor, the two of you need to make a deal. With a sub, the process is simple: You both sign the bid to make it binding. Then, when the job is complete, have the sub sign a lien waiver (the forms are available at most stationery stores) while you write out a check to pay for the job.

With a GC you may need a more elaborate contract. Usually the GC will present you with a standard version he or she uses often. Read it carefully. If there are clauses you don't understand, check with an attorney. Here are some points that should be covered.

- Start and completion dates. Try to include penalties if the work isn't finished on time. On the other hand, the cost could go up if

Building inspections are required to assure that all work has been done to code. Local requirements may vary, but most areas require inspections of the framing, plumbing, wiring, insulation, and drywall, plus a final inspection.

you cause a delay.

- A payment schedule. Typically this calls for 30 percent up front, 30 percent when the work is about half done, and 30 percent after all work has been completed, inspected, and approved. Withholding the final 10 percent for 30 days gives you time to be sure the work was done right – and motivates the contractor to promptly fix any items on your punch list.
- Change orders. What will it cost if you change the plan or specifications? Any change orders should be in writing and initialed by both parties.
- Lien waivers. These ensure that the contractor has paid all subcontractors and suppliers. Make sure you will receive a signed lien waiver from the GC as well as one from each sub and supplier who provided labor or material to your job.
- Code compliance. Any contract should specify that all work conform to local building codes.

Permits

Don't, under any circumstances, decide to forget about permits and do the work behind closed doors. You might get away with it, but if you're caught, you could end up paying a fine plus the cost of having everything torn out and done over again. Also, if illegally installed wiring, for example, causes a fire, your homeowner's insurance company might deny your claim.

Post your permit and inspection record where an inspector can easily refer to them. We like to store the papers in a sealable, plastic bag. That protects them from the elements and keeps all the documents together.

Logistics

You've set a budget, finalized a plan, and applied for a building permit, but a few key questions remain to be answered. What are you going to do with demolition and construction debris? When should you take delivery of materials, where are you going to store them, and how are you going to get them into the house? Developing a plan of attack minimizes unpleasant surprises later on.

Good riddance

Most communities won't haul away construction debris, which means you have to figure out a way to dispose of it yourself. One option is to rent a demolition dumpster. These get dumped at special landfills that accept only construction materials, so their dumping fees can be about half what you pay at a regular landfill. Demolition debris is heavy, so locate the dumpster as close to the house as possible. Keep in mind, though, that setting a dumpster on an asphalt driveway will leave serious divots, and setting it on the lawn may kill the grass. If you don't mind lugging heavy stuff over long distances, consider parking the dumpster in the street. Check with the police department first, though. Some communities don't allow it at all, others charge a fee. It may be even cheaper to just let debris pile up in the garage or driveway and have a hauling service cart it away at the end of the job.

Also, find out if you can recycle some of the stuff you tear out. Some communities have programs that accept used fixtures and

Plan ahead. *Because the walls and door were already in place when this shower stall arrived, it had to be hefted over a deck railing, onto scaffolding, and through the bathroom window.*

building materials and make them available to people doing low-cost renovation work.

If your project requires removing materials that contain asbestos or lead, hire a licensed abatement contractor to do the job. Any abatement contractor you hire should give you a certificate stating the material removed from your house was disposed of according to local regulations.

Ordering materials

You'll find most of the construction materials needed for your project are in stock at the local home center, but custom cabinets, plumbing fixtures, faucets, and tile will need to be special-ordered. Check lead times and build them into your schedule.

Staging materials

When all your materials arrive, you need to know where you're going to store them. An attached garage provides a secure, sheltered place to stow materials and fixtures. It also makes a nice workspace for fabricating countertops and cutting resilient flooring. If you don't have an attached garage, try to dedicate a room near the bathroom to be a staging area. Be sure to protect the floors and walls with drop cloths so they don't get damaged as you move materials around.

A final point to consider is insurance. Call your agent and ask if stored building materials are covered. Chances are, they aren't. Most homeowners' policies only cover materials once they are attached to the house. If that's the case with your policy, and you're storing high-end fixtures and materials, look into buying additional coverage until the job is done.

How long will it take?

Here's a time-line for a typical remodel in which no major surprises are discovered.

- Demolition. One long weekend.
- Rough-ins. One day each for carpentry, plumbing, and wiring.
- Closing up walls and ceilings. You can hang drywall in a bathroom in a day, but mudding the seams must span three days to allow for drying time between coats.
- Tile and flooring. Plan a weekend for setting and grouting wall tiles, another for ceramic tile flooring. You can install resilient tile and sheet flooring in a single day.
- Prime and paint. Two days.
- Finish work. Setting cabinets, fixtures, mirrors, and other components will probably take another couple of days.

PRODUCT SELECTION

If you're like most people, *you've been clipping out pictures of bathrooms ever since you were hit with the urge to remodel. Now, head to the home center to pick up product literature, color chips, and samples of items you like.*

At home, spread everything out and start experimenting with the different pieces. Which combination of colors, textures, and finishes looks best to you? Which price tags fit your budget? Gradually you'll find yourself gravitating toward the combination of products that will look and work best in your bathroom.

Lavatories

To a plumber or a fixture dealer, sinks are strictly for kitchens and laundries, while lavatories are for bathrooms. Most people use the words interchangeably, though – and regardless of what you choose to call them, there's a huge selection to choose from. Sinks come in a broad range of shapes, sizes, materials, colors, and with a variety of mounting systems.

Material differences

What a sink is made of determines how long it will last and, to some extent, its price. Here are the main contenders.

- Vitreous china. These sinks are heavy, easy to clean, and last almost indefinitely. China sinks will even stand up to abrasive cleansers. They can crack or chip, however, if you drop a heavy object on one.

- Enameled cast iron. Cast-iron sinks are also long-lasting sinks. While enamel is pretty tough, abrasive cleaners will eventually dull the finish, and it can chip if sharp or heavy objects are dropped on it.

- Solid-surface material. Made of either acrylic or polyester, solid-surface material is available in many colors and stone patterns which can be mixed and matched to create integral sinks and countertops. Solid-surface material is long-lasting and easy to clean. Scratches and stains can usually be buffed out.

- Cultured marble. Yes, there really is powdered marble mixed in with the polyester resin. Because it's porous, cultured marble is finished with a gel coat that can be left glossy or buffed out to a satin finish. High-end versions are sometimes referred to as cast-polymer or molded marble. These have a thicker gel coat that is less prone to cracking and crazing.

Sizing a sink

With sinks, bigger is better. For comfort (and to minimize splashing), choose the largest one that will fit into your bathroom. Oval and rectangular basins use available space more efficiently than round basins.

To install two sinks in the same counter, allow at least 30 inches between the basin's centers and 15 inches between each basin's center and the end of the countertop.

Universal design considerations

Wall-hung and pedestal sinks are more accessible than standard vanity sinks. They should be installed no more than 34 inches above the floor. Covering the hot-water supply line and drain line protects against burns. For a countertop installation, look for a sink that is shallow enough to allow knee space underneath.

Pedestal sinks

A pedestal sink is a good choice for a powder room – which typically requires little storage space – or for a larger bathroom where storage space is provided by a linen closet or cabinet.

Pedestal sinks are mounted on a wall bracket which is an-

chored to blocking behind the wall; the pedestal is not the primary sink support.

These sinks are made almost exclusively of vitreous china and are available in a variety of styles, from traditional to ultra-modern.

Product

Self-rimming

Flush-mount

Undermount

Integral

Wall-hung

Barrier-free

Features	Upkeep	Installation notes
A self-rimming, or drop-in, sink has a raised, rounded rim that rests on the countertop. The height of the rim helps minimize the amount of water splashing onto the counter. This is the easiest style of bathroom sink to install.	Because the raised rim contains splashing, you need to wipe fewer water spots from the counter around a self-rimming sink. Maintain the bead of caulk around the rim to prevent water seepage.	Installing a self-rimming sink is a straightforward procedure. Lay a bead of caulk around the opening in the countertop, set the sink onto the caulk, and make the plumbing connections.
The rim of a flush-mounted sink rests flush with the countertop. The gap between the two is bridged by a metal rim. The tile-in sink is similar, except its edge is flush with the countertop tile. It has no metal ring.	The rim around the edge tends to collect grime, and splashing leaves puddles and water spots on the countertop.	You have to temporarily support the sink in the opening while you tighten bolts through clips under the counter. With a flush-mounted sink, be sure to caulk where the rim meets the countertop and the basin.
Undermount sinks rest entirely below the countertop. The cutout for the sink is a little smaller than the basin so that the countertop slightly overhangs the sink. These sinks work well with solid-surface countertops.	Cleaning counters is a breeze – with no lip in the way, you just push everything into the sink. But cleaning the hard-to-get-at joint between the counter and an undermount sink can be a hassle.	An undermount sink installs almost the same as a flush-mounted model. Again, the key is to temporarily hold the sink in place while you attach the basin to the underside of the counter. (See page 33 to learn how to make a temporary support for undermount sinks.)
Integral units combine a sink and countertop into one tightly seamed or molded piece. They are available in both cultured marble and solid-surface material. Sinks and countertops of the same color or contrasting colors can be seamed together.	Splashing can be a problem, but again, you just mop toward the sink, then wipe out the basin. There are no joints where debris can stick. Use only mild non-abrasive cleaners on solid surface and cultured marble.	Installing an integral sink and counter is an easy two-person job. You simply glue it to the top edges of the vanity cabinet. Custom-fabricated solid-surface sinks/countertops are often installed by the fabricator.
Wall-hung sinks are mounted to a bracket attached to the wall studs. They're available in a range of styles and colors. Some have support legs at the front; others are available with a matching cover to conceal the pipes.	The sink itself is as easy as any other to clean. However, without a surrounding countertop, all splashes end up on the floor and walls.	A wall-hung sink gets mounted on a special bracket which is secured to blocking or studs behind the drywall. Installation is easier (and safer) if there are 2x4 props and an extra set of hands to support the sink while maneuvering it over the bracket.
Countertop sinks that provide wheelchair access usually have shallow bowls and offset drains that free up knee space underneath. Wall-hung sinks also provide wheelchair access and can be mounted at any desired height.	The same as other wall-hung or countertop sinks.	Barrier-free sinks are simply wall-hung, pedestal, or variations of self-rimming models; install them as you would any other sink. Exposed drains and hot-water supply pipes should be covered to prevent burns.

Fittings

With fittings, quality is usually determined by the quantity of brass inside. An assembly made entirely of brass resists corrosion best.

Steer clear of cheap fittings. Repairs could be frequent and parts all but impossible to find. It's smart to check on the availability of replacement parts before you buy any faucet – especially those that come from an unknown manufacturer or have an unusual design.

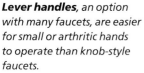

Lever handles, an option with many faucets, are easier for small or arthritic hands to operate than knob-style faucets.

Shower faucets

Pressure-balancing valves are typically available in shower faucets. They help prevent sudden temperature changes when the pressure in a shower supply line drops due to a line being opened somewhere else in the house. The pressure balancing valve senses pressure changes and reacts to maintain a constant temperature – even if someone flushes a toilet or starts a dishwasher. When the pressure in one line drops, it decreases pressure in the opposite line, maintaining the preset temperature and serving as a safety against scalding. Some also feature a switch you can use to limit the maximum temperature at which the valve can be set.

Showerheads

Low-flow showerheads flow at no more than 2.5 gallons per minute (gpm), which saves both water and the energy needed to heat it. Many also let you control the volume and/or adjust the spray in increments from a pulsating stream to a gentle mist.

Hand-held showerheads offer the greatest range of uses. Look for one that slides on a vertical bar so each member of the family can set it to a comfortable height.

Single-lever faucets are available with and without escutcheon plates. Those without escutcheons must be mounted on sinks with a single-hole drilling. Single-lever faucets with escutcheon plates can be mounted in either single hole or centerset drillings.

A centerset faucet fits onto a three-hole sink that has 4 inches between the holes for the hot- and cold-water valves. Many faucets are available in both a centerset and a widespread configuration. Likewise, most sinks are available drilled in single hole, centerset, and widespread configurations. Make sure the faucet and sink you select are compatible.

Install a widespread faucet on a three-hole sink that has 8 inches between the outer holes. Larger sinks and pedestal sinks are usually drilled for widespread faucets. Widespread faucets can also be mounted directly on countertops, usually in combination with an undermount sink or a drop-in basin without any faucet drillings.

Toilets

Low-flush toilets are now the standard (not to mention the law) in the United States. Switching to low-flush toilets can reduce water usage for a family of four by up to 11,000 gallons of water a year. This saves on water bills and takes a big load off sewage treatment facilities and septic systems.

Specialty toilets

You're probably familiar with the basic toilet styles: one-piece and two-piece toilets with round or elongated bowls. But there are a few other options you may be less familiar with.

- A wall-hung toilet flushes out the back of the bowl instead of the bottom. It's much easier to mop the floor around a wall-hung toilet, but you'll pay a premium for the convenience.
- Short on space? A toilet with a triangular tank tucks neatly into a corner.
- Toilets with 17- to 19-inch rim heights meet the needs of people who use wheelchairs. Tall people also find them more comfortable to use.

One-piece toilets integrate the tank and bowl into a seamless, space-saving unit. They flush more quietly than models with a separate tank. They are also more expensive than two-piece models.

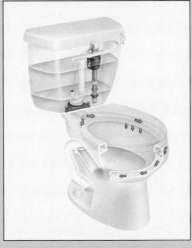

Elongated bowl toilets are considered more comfortable by most adults. However, they take up more space and cost a bit more, too. Designed to UD specifications, this one has a 17½ inch rim height (about two inches taller than a standard toilet).

The low-down on low-flush

No doubt about it, early low-flush toilets were universally disliked by homeowners. They clogged frequently, streaked easily, and often had to be flushed twice. We've even heard rumors that a black market of sorts developed for old 3.5- and 5-gallon toilets.

Fortunately, the manufacturers sent their engineers back to their drawing boards. Resulting improvements include an increased water surface in the bowl (less streaking), more and better-positioned jets (fewer double flushes), and glazed traps (less clogging).

There are two different low-flush systems: pressure-assisted and gravity-fed. Pressure-assisted toilets are more efficient than gravity-fed models, but they're also more expensive, prone to streaking, and much noisier. Flushing one at night could wake up others in the household. The gravity-fed system operates like a traditional toilet. Gravity-fed toilets cost half to one-quarter as much as pressurized models.

A gravity-fed toilet relies on the pressure of water leaving the tank to create a siphon that forces waste out of the bowl and through the trap. Rim jets and a siphon jet help accelerate the flow of water and waste through the trap.

A pressure-assisted toilet uses the pressure of the incoming water supply to compress air in a reservoir within the tank. When you flush, the compressed air propels water through the bowl at high speed to clear the bowl in seconds.

First the resurfacer acid-etches the existing surface, fills any scratches, dings, and dents, and sands down the whole tub.

Next comes a bonding coat that serves as a primer for the glaze coat.

Finally, at least three layers of glaze coat are applied. The finish should be cured and ready to use in 24 to 48 hours.

Tubs

Bathtubs come in many sizes, shapes, styles, and colors, but they're made of just four different materials: cast iron, acrylic, fiberglass, and enameled steel. Here's how they compare.

Cast iron, finished with a tough coating of enamel, makes a tub that's heavy, durable, quiet, and heat-retentive. Cast-iron tubs can last almost indefinitely if you're careful to avoid scratching or chipping the finish.

Acrylic tubs are fiberglass reinforced. These tubs are light, durable, and stain-resistant. Scratches can usually be sanded out. (Buff afterward to restore the shine.)

Steel tubs are inexpensive and lightweight. But steel tubs also are noisy and don't hold heat well; if you decide to go with one, muffle it with fiberglass insulation before you install it. The finish of a steel tub wears off over time, which leads to rusting.

Fiberglass tubs are often combined with an integral shower surround. The size of a one-piece tub and surround makes it difficult to maneuver through doorways, so consider a panelized unit for remodel situations. Unless care is taken to avoid abrasive cleaners, the gel-coat finish will become burnished and dull. Deep scratches may go through the color layer, revealing a different-color base.

Plan ahead

While most plumbing fixtures aren't installed until the end of a remodel, the tub must go in early. Tubs get attached to the studs before the tub surround – whether fiberglass or ceramic tile – is installed.

The other reason to arrange early delivery of a tub is maneuverability. In a bathroom addition, it's easier to set the tub into position before all the studs are in place and the walls closed up. In a remodel situation, measure carefully to make sure the new tub will fit through the doorways and up (or down) any stairs.

A self-rimming tub gets set into a platform. Usually you need to specify whether you need a left- or right-hand drain. Here, the drain is in the center.

Alcove tubs – the most typical tub configuration – are designed to fit into a recess with walls on three sides. Locating the faucet at the edge of the tub makes it more accessible.

Vintage reproduction tubs are often as deep as the original versions, allowing most people to comfortably soak in water up to their chins. This version rests on a special base; others have claw feet.

Shower Stalls

Creating a shower in your new bathroom can be as simple as adding doors to the bathtub. The most common style is the by-pass door – two doors that slide in a frame mounted to the tub's endwalls. The other side, trackless doors, have no top or bottom tracks; the doors retract and pivot to allow full access to the tub area. With either type you will have a choice of glass styles and hardware finishes.

Shapes for stand-alone shower stalls include square, rectangular, corner, angled, and curved. In addition to the shape and size of the base, you will need to know what thresh-

A one-piece molded-fiberglass tub/shower or shower stall that is properly installed will never leak or rust. To prevent cracking, you should provide framing at all stress points. Prefab stalls range in size from a compact 32 inches square up to 48 by 34 inches.

This neo-angle corner shower combines a glass and aluminum shower enclosure with custom-tiled back walls. Options include a seat and a deep shower pan for foot baths.

A custom shower can be shaped to fit any available space. Generally, a comfortable minimum is 36 inches square. Popular amenities include multiple showerheads, built-in benches, and wall niches for shampoo and towels.

old you want. (Threshold is the number of sides that will be enclosed by the glass sides and door.) A single threshold is designed to fit in an alcove with walls on three sides, a double threshold tucks into a corner with glass on the other two sides, and a triple-threshold base has a wall on one side only, with glass sides and a door on the other three sides. It'll be easier to choose a compatible base and enclosure if you stick with one manufacturer for both parts.

This barrier-free shower includes a fold-down seat, grab bars, a low threshold, and an adjustable-height hand-held shower. Locate the faucet (which should have a pressure-balancing valve) so it's within reach of a seated person as well as accessible from outside the shower.

Flooring

Bathroom floors take a lot of abuse. They have to put up with heavy traffic, steam, humidity, splashes, standing water, and frequent scrubbings. Consider how the flooring you choose will stand up to this treatment. Weigh that against how the flooring will feel underfoot (some people find ceramic tile cold, for example) and how slippery it will be when it's wet.

Just as important as the finish material is the surface underneath; an unstable underlayment will cause the new floor to wear prematurely, and could void the manufacturer's warranty, as well. If the old flooring is in

Ceramic tile is a great choice for bathroom floors. If properly installed and maintained, a ceramic tile floor can last a lifetime, even under the wet conditions typical in most bathrooms

	Sheet vinyl	Vinyl tile	Ceramic tile
Product			
Features	Because sheet vinyl comes in 6-, 9-, and 12-foot widths, you can avoid seams in all but a very large bathroom.	Vinyl tile is generally less expensive than sheet vinyl but the thicker the tile, the more you'll pay. You can create your own geometric patterns by combining different colors of tile.	Given the wide selection of colors, sizes, and shapes, you can create just about any design you like with ceramic tile. Costs for ceramic tile range from moderate to very pricey.
Upkeep	No-wax vinyl wipes clean with a damp mop and mild detergent. The life span of a sheet vinyl floor depends on the quality you pay for, but 10 to 15 years is typical.	Vinyl tile cleans easily with a damp mop, but the seams tend to collect dirt. The seams may also allow standing water to seep through to the underlayment below.	Routine cleaning just calls for damp-mopping with mild detergent. You will need to reseal the grout about once a year.
Installation notes	The installation method depends on the type of vinyl. Fully adhered vinyl requires adhesive under the entire sheet; perimeter bonded vinyl is glued down only along the edges.	Self-stick floor tiles were one of the first building materials specifically designed for do-it-yourself installation. Dry-back tiles have to be set in adhesive; for easier installation, choose self-stick tiles.	Installing ceramic tile is more work than installing sheet vinyl or vinyl tiles, but it is still a feasible – and satisfying – do-it-yourself project.

good condition, you may be able to install the new floor right on top of the old. In most cases you will need to add a new underlayment first. For vinyl flooring, use ¼-inch-thick lauan. For ceramic tile, install new cement backer board. However, before you decide to install new flooring over old, figure out how much it will raise the floor height. Adding backer board and ceramic tile could raise the floor height significantly. Code allows for only a ¼-inch height change where two floorings meet. You can usually install a beveled threshold to ease the transition, but you may also have to trim down the door.

***Resilient sheet flooring** is available in a wide selection of colors and patterns that often mimic the look of other flooring materials such as tile, stone, or wood – at a fraction of the price.*

Wood	Marble	Carpet
Wood is a poor choice for bathroom flooring. It simply won't stand up to the water and humidity. This doesn't mean that you have to give up the look of wood in your bathroom, though.	Half-inch-thick marble tiles come in many colors, shadings, and veining patterns. Though not as astronomically expensive as it once was, marble is still a costly flooring material.	Woven from synthetic fibers, bathroom carpeting is warm underfoot and cuts down on noise – but it's not a good material for high-splash areas.
Vinyl woodgrain planks look like the real thing, yet are impervious to moisture, mildew, and other enemies of solid wood. It comes in 3- by 36-inch strips.	Marble stains easily unless it's sealed. Regular cleaning, resealing, and polishing are necessary to keep a marble floor in top condition. Like ceramic tile, marble lasts almost indefinitely.	Prone to moisture, mildew, and stains, carpeting is a high-maintenance bathroom flooring material. Confine its use to areas such as a powder room or the lavatory area of a master bathroom.
Vinyl planks are installed and maintained like vinyl tiles.	Marble tiles are tricky to work with, and installing them is best hired out to professionals, especially when you consider this material's high cost per square foot.	Some types of carpeting can be installed by do-it-yourselfers; others carry warranties that are based on professional installation.

Creature comforts

Stepping barefoot onto a cold floor is no way to ease into the day. If the budget allows, consider installing a radiant heating system under your new bathroom floor. There are electric systems ideal for retrofitting a bathroom. With these systems, heating wires (sometimes woven into a mat) are embedded in a thin layer of concrete or placed just under the flooring. A separate thermostat controls the system.

Countertops

Even the simplest, most basic bathroom remodeling is likely to include replacing the countertop, regardless of whether or not you plan to replace the vanity cabinet underneath it. Your old countertop may look like it's a permanent part of the cabinet, but it's most likely held in place with just a few screws or dabs of glue. You just disconnect the sink, lift off the old top, and set a new one in its place.

Safety

A countertop color that contrasts with the floor color, or one that is edge-banded with an accent color, makes it easier for a visually impaired person (or anyone, for that matter) to determine where the edge of the counter is.

Product	Features	Upkeep	Construction notes
Laminate	Plastic-laminate countertops consist of 1/16-inch-thick laminate bonded to a particleboard substrate. Laminates come in lots of colors, patterns, and textures, many of them imitating more expensive materials.	Laminate cleans easily with dish soap and water or with mild cleansers. Over the years laminate dulls and wears thin, and hard blows can chip or dent it. Color-through laminates are more expensive but show fewer scratches and dings.	Postformed laminate tops have integral backsplashes and rounded edges. You can also order a custom-made counter or build your own. Install laminate counters by driving screws up through cabinet corner brackets into the counter.
Ceramic tile	Tile makes a durable countertop that will last for years and years – and the design possibilities are almost endless. It costs more per square foot than laminate.	Tile has a long life span if properly installed and maintained. Provide a solid substrate to avoid cracked tiles and grout joints. Avoid abrasive cleansers. Grout joints will need occasional scrubbing with bleach water. Reseal grout yearly.	Most competent do-it-yourselfers can handle laying a tile countertop. You bond backer board to particleboard, lay the tiles, and grout between them. For the best looking job, pay close attention to tile layout.
Solid-surface	Available as ready-made counters with integral sinks or custom-fabricated to your specifications, solid-surface material often mimics natural stone. Cost ranges from moderate to very expensive.	Solid-surface counters clean easily with soap and water or with a mild, non-abrasive cleaner. Stains and scratches can be removed with fine-grade sandpaper. (Get directions from the solid-surface manufacturer before you try this.)	While there are some solid-surface countertops available prefabricated at home centers, most have to be ordered through custom fabricators who also do the installation. Ready-made tops get glued to the vanity cabinet.
Cultured marble	Made from chips of natural marble embedded in polyester resin, cultured marble comes in standard counter dimensions, with or without an integral sink. High-end versions are sometimes called cast-polymer or molded marble.	Cultured marble is very durable and easy to maintain. It's prone to scratches, so avoid abrasive cleaners. Higher-end products have a thicker gel-coat that better resists crazing and cracking.	Glue a cultured marble countertop to the top of the vanity cabinet with silicone adhesive. If there is an integral sink, mount the faucet before installing the countertop.

Lighting

Good bathroom lighting includes two types of lighting. Ambient lighting provides the general light, while task lighting provides bright and focused light for specific areas of the room.

Ambient lighting

Ceiling fixtures usually provide the ambient light in a bathroom. Try to create a light level of 30 lumens per square foot of floor space (about 4 watts of incandescent light or 2 watts of fluorescent light per square foot).

In a large bathroom, don't rely on vanity lights to provide the ambient light; that will cause too much glare. Plus, you need ambient light to even out shadows cast by task lights around the vanity.

A fixture installed above the mirror must be carefully positioned to avoid casting harsh shadows on the face. Choose a multi-light fixture at least 24 inches long. Mount it at a height of 78 inches.

Task lighting

In a bathroom most task lighting is around the mirror. These fixtures should provide diffuse, non-glaring light that illuminates the person at the mirror (not the mirror itself). The light should be strong enough see details, but not intense. It's best to place fixtures to the sides of the mirror.

Specialty lighting

Providing light for special uses occasionally requires additional fixtures, but is often as simple as adding dimmer switches for the ambient fixtures. Dimming the lights to a low level at night, for example, will be appreciated by all sleepy-eyed middle-of-the night bathroom visitors.

Put a fixture over the bathtub on a dimmer switch to accommodate those who want to read in the tub as well as those who just want to lay back and relax. In shower stalls install watertight shower lights with shatterproof diffuser lenses.

Light the inside of the linen closet by aiming a bathroom ceiling fixture so it shines into the linen closet. Or you can install a closet light with a door jamb switch that is activated by opening and closing the closet door.

Lights on either side of a mirror create even lighting and cancel out shadows from other light fixtures. Install the fixtures 60 inches high and space them at least 28 inches apart.

Fluorescent lighting and bathrooms

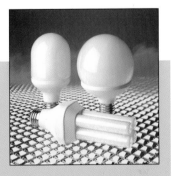

Until recently, fluorescent lights were not a good choice for lighting bathrooms because they cast greenish light, making just about anyone look sickly, and making it almost impossible to apply makeup.

Now fluorescent bulbs are available in a variety of light colors, from cool white to warm white, making them suitable for use in bathrooms. Compact fluorescent bulbs, in particular, are often used in recessed can lights.

Compact fluorescent bulbs come in many shapes, sizes, and wattages. Many of them contain a ballast in the base of the bulb, so you can use them in fixtures with standard-size sockets without using an adapter. Look for bulbs with electronic ballasts; they are smaller than magnetic ballasts, can power higher wattage bulbs, and turn on instantly without flickering.

On the downside, most fluorescent bulbs cannot be used in fixtures with dimmer switches. Also, they do contain mercury and should be disposed of properly.

Surface-mounted *medicine cabinets are the best option if there are pipes behind the lavatory or if your remodeling plans don't include opening up the walls. Many medicine cabinets have coordinated or integral lighting fixtures.*

An old idea *that's new again: Hot water circulates through this antique-repro-duction towel warmer. You turn it on and off with a valve at lower right.*

Scrutinize your floor plan to see if a new linen cabinet or additional vanity cabinets can be worked in somewhere. Stock bathroom cabinets come in many sizes. Sink bases range from 24- to 48-inches wide and come in many door and drawer configurations. Some cabinet lines also include matching wall, linen, and medicine cabinets. Linen cabinets are usually 18-inches wide; matching medicine cabinets come 24-, 30-, or 36-inches wide.

Cabinets and Accessories

Bathrooms, like kitchens, have accumulated an astonishing array of small appliances in the past two decades. Unless you're partial to cluttered counters and towels hung over the shower door, carefully evaluate your storage needs before selecting cabinets and hardware.

Cabinets

The main difference between kitchen and bathroom cabinets is size – vanity cabinets are shorter and not as deep. The styles are often the same, though. There's no reason not to use a kitchen cabinet in a bathroom; an appliance garage can hide a hair dryer as well as it does a toaster. Other popular cabinet upgrades and accessories can also be put to good use in a bathroom, including roll-out trays, tilt-out bins, and trim moldings.

Signs of quality cabinetry include dovetailed or doweled joints in the drawer boxes, ball bearing drawer glides, adjustable hinges, and well finished interiors with adjustable shelves.

Accessories

Bathroom accessories are available in a variety of materials, including porcelain, vitreous china, brass, and steel. Polished brass is one of the most popular choices – look for pieces that are lacquered to prevent tarnishing. With chrome or nickel finishes, choose pieces with a brass base.

Don't plan on using towel bars as grab bars. To be effective, grab bars must be strong and securely anchored. Look for grab bars made of solid brass tubing, welded stainless steel, or brazed solid brass.

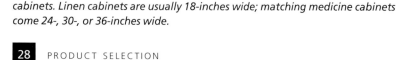

Bathroom accessories are both functional and decorative. For a unified look, choose accessories with the same finish and style.

DEMOLITION

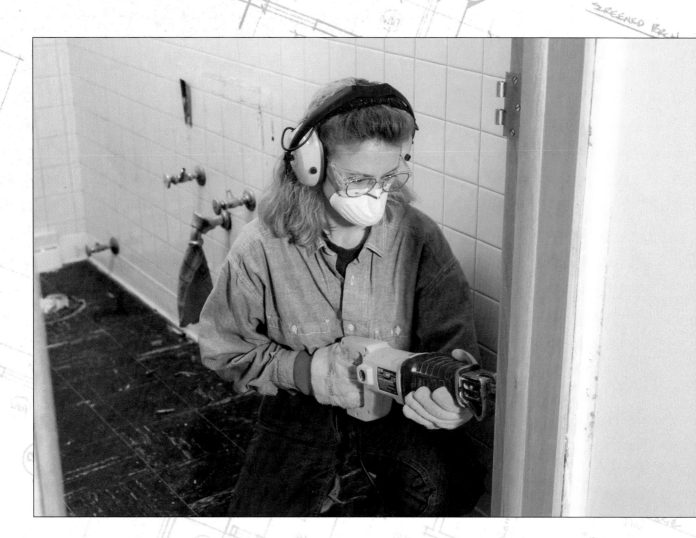

Some people think demolition is fun*. That's debatable. Tearing out an old bathroom is hard, messy work, and hauling out the heavy debris will leave you with sore muscles screaming for a hot bath – and the sad realization that the bathtub is now in the driveway.*

Whether you think it's fun or not, you can't deny that demolition is exciting. Once begun, the process moves quickly, change is immediately apparent, and there is no turning back. If you're expanding into adjoining space, demolition also provides the first glimpse of how the new room will look and feel.

Safety First

Demolition has its dangers. After all, you're working with water and electricity, bulky fixtures, dusty debris, and several materials that could pose hazards to your health. To prevent mishaps – and maybe even a trip to the emergency room – take these precautions.

Shut off the water

Even if the fixtures in your bathroom have stop valves to cut off the water, it's best to shut down and drain the entire supply system. Why? Because in the process of tearing out tile and drywall or plaster, you could accidentally damage a stop or the pipe leading to it. Water from a ruptured stop or pipe can do a lot of damage in just a few minutes.

First, close your home's main valve; it's probably right next to the water meter or by the pressurized storage tank, if you have well water. Then, to drain water that's still in the system, open up both the highest and lowest faucets in the house.

If you cut into any pipes during demolition, you'll need to cap them before you turn the water back on.

Shut off the electricity

Unless you have a whirlpool tub (which has its own circuit), chances are good that your bathroom has just one circuit, probably shared with a nearby bedroom.

If the breakers or fuses in your main electrical panel are labeled, you're in luck. If they're unlabeled, or you don't trust the labeling, plug a radio into a bathroom outlet and turn it up so you can hear it down at the electrical panel. Now start turning off breakers. When the noise stops, you've found the right circuit.

Hazardous materials

Asbestos and lead have been banned from most building materials since the late 1970s, but still lurk in many homes built prior to that time. If you suspect your house contains either of these hazards, check with your local health department or EPA office. They can recommend test labs and abatement companies. Here's where to look for these contaminants.

Asbestos

Houses built between 1930 and 1950 may contain asbestos insulation around steam and hot water pipes. Textured paint and patching compounds made before 1977 often contain asbestos. And pre-1977 resilient tiles and sheet flooring often have asbestos fibers in their backings.

The danger from asbestos is airborne fibers. Fibers become airborne when asbestos-containing materials are sanded, sawed, broken, or shredded. When inhaled, the fibers lodge in the lungs where they can cause diseases that may not appear for many years.

Lead paint

Lead pigments were widely used in oil-based paints before 1978. Lead paint was often

---

Watch your step

Protect floors with heavy paper such as kraft paper or resin paper. Tape it down with duct tape so it doesn't slip. Better yet, buy some reusable canvas dropcloths. Don't use plastic or newspapers; they're too slippery and could cause you to fall.

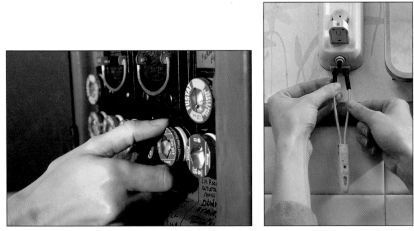

Shut off power to the bathroom before starting demolition. After you've shut down a circuit, tape a warning on the panel so no one turns it back on while you're working. To be sure a circuit is dead, test each of the outlets, switches, and light fixtures with a neon tester (above, right). To test receptacles, insert one probe in each slot. With fixtures, loosen the fixture and test the wire ends. If the tester glows, there's still power.

Close the main valve to shut down your home's water system. If there are two valves at the meter, turn off either one. To drain all the water from the pipes, open both the highest and the lowest faucets in the house.

used on trim moldings and in kitchens, bathrooms, and laundry areas.

While chipping and peeling lead paint is an obvious problem, lead dust is particularly troublesome because you can't see it, and because it passes right through the filters of regular vacuum cleaners and shop vacs. Surfaces that rub against one another (window sashes, frames, and sills, for example, or doors and frames) are a major source of lead dust.

Never scrape or sand lead paint. Also avoid heat-melting lead paint since that vaporizes the lead.

Over time, ingesting or inhaling lead can cause lowered IQ, learning disabilities, and behavioral disorders. Children under six, and especially fetuses, are particularly at risk.

Wear protective clothing

Obviously, you're not going to dress for demolition in your Sunday best, but for safety's sake, there's more to it than that.

Jeans, long-sleeved shirts, and heavy work gloves protect against scratches. If you don't have sturdy work boots, buy a pair; nails can easily pierce lightweight shoes or sneakers.

Masks, hearing protectors, and safety glasses complete the uniform for most demolition jobs, but if you'll be tearing out a ceiling, round out your wardrobe with a hard hat.

Finally, leave all your jewelry on the dresser. It's too easy to snag a ring, watch, or bracelet and cause a painful injury.

Proper demolition gear *includes eye, ear, and lung protection, work gloves and boots, jeans, and long sleeves.*

Breathe easy

For ordinary demolition, use a particulate respirator. Look for one approved by the National Institute for Occupational Safety and Health (NIOSH). This organization tests and certifies masks and respirators for specific hazardous substances. The best particulate respirators have a NIOSH approval number that begins with the sequence TC-84A, indicating it has passed rigorous testing.

Cartridge respirators only work for specific gases, vapors, or particulates. Using the wrong one won't protect you. Always read the packaging when selecting a respirator. It will say whether the cartridges are for particulates (including dust, fumes, and mists), gases, or vapors. It will often give examples of the types of jobs it's approved for.

Try on the respirator before you buy. If it doesn't fit tightly against your face, it will offer little (if any) protection because air and contaminants will be pulled in around the edges as you inhale.

All masks and respirators have some resistance to air flow, making your lungs work a little harder. For most people, this is hardly noticeable, but if you have respiratory problems, check with your doctor before using a mask or respirator.

Be sure to ventilate your work area even when wearing a respirator. Too high a concentration of contaminant can overwhelm the respirator – and you. A box fan pointed out an open window works well.

Planning and Preparation

Order of events

It's usually quickest and easiest to dismantle a bathroom in roughly the reverse order it was built. That way you won't waste time trying to work around items that are in your way.

Start by removing the millwork and hardware, then pull the sink, toilet, and cabinets. With all those items out of the way, there will be room to remove the tub. Next take down drywall so you have access to any plumbing and wiring that is going to be rerouted. Finally, rip out the framing for any walls you plan to move, then tackle the flooring.

Cover doorways with plastic to confine dust to the construction area. Zippered openings allow easy access to the work area. With these, you fasten plastic over the entry, tape the zippers to the plastic, then slit open the plastic behind the zippers.

Before you pick up the sledge hammer, take a look around to see what's worth saving. Millwork, for example, probably matches other moldings in your home, and you might want to sell or reuse hardware or vintage light fixtures.

Containing dust

To keep most of the dust contained to the work area, seal doorways with plastic. Use overlapping sheets of plastic weighted down with scrap 2x4s or get a zippered plastic door kit.

Cover heating or cooling registers with plastic and turn off the furnace fan if possible. Dust that gets into your home's ductwork will soon be everywhere.

Removing millwork

To remove millwork, start by slipping the curved end of a prybar behind a corner and prying gently. After you've loosened a few inches, wedge the molding away from the wall with a shim. Now move along, prying and wedging as you go.

Removing hardware

Remove hardware that's attached with screws by loosening the set-screw in the escutcheon plate. The only way to remove hardware that has been glued to the wall is to snap it free and repair the damage later.

If a mirror is glued to the wall, chances are good it'll break. To be safe, drape the mirror with a drop cloth and clip it along the edges as the mirror comes free of the wall.

Creating a disposal path

If your bathroom has a window that overlooks the driveway, consider removing the sashes, protecting the jambs and sills, and improvising a chute so you can slide debris directly into a dumpster or truck. If the path must go through the house, choose the shortest route and line it with drop cloths so you won't scratch the floors.

Loosen millwork with a prybar, starting at the corner. If your prybar gouges the wall surface, slip a taping knife behind it.

Pull nails from the back with a nail puller if you're planning to reuse the millwork. Don't try to push them out, that might damage the wood.

Remove a medicine cabinet by loosening the screws that secure it to the surrounding studs. Hang onto the mirror as you remove the last screw and let the cabinet tip out of the wall.

Removing Fixtures

Even if you're planning to keep your current fixtures, it might be worth the effort to pull them out now. It will keep them from being damaged during the renovation and you'll be grateful for the extra work space, especially if you're replacing the tub. However, if you're keeping the tub, be sure to cover it with plywood or heavy drop cloths to protect against scratches.

Be prepared to replace an old toilet if you do pull it out. Low-flush models are required for all new installations, and local codes may also require you to replace the old toilet if you pull it.

Pulling a sink

No matter how a sink is mounted, you follow the same basic procedure to dismantle it: disconnect the supply lines, remove the trap, and muscle out the basin.

To remove a flush-mount sink, remove the screws or lug bolts that clamp it to the underside of the vanity top. If your basin is a self-rimming model that's adhered to the vanity top, cut the adhesive with a utility knife and lift the sink free.

With an integral (one-piece) sink/vanity top, look for screws underneath each corner of the top. Some integral units are glued to the top edge of the cabinet.

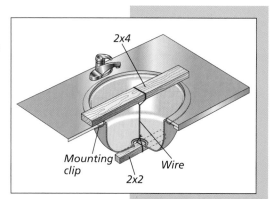

1 *Close the fixture stops,* then disconnect the compression nuts that join the lines to the fixture stops. A bucket catches the drips.

2 *Slip nuts* connect the trap to the lavatory's tailpiece and to the elbow that sticks out from the wall. Loosen the slip nuts with groove-joint pliers, then tip the water from the trap into the bucket.

3 *Stuff a rag* into the lavatory drain pipe to keep sewer gas from backing up into the bathroom.

4 *Remove a wall-hung sink* by lifting it off the wall bracket and front legs. Make sure someone's nearby to catch the legs.

Removing an undermount sink

If possible, remove the countertop and sink together. Otherwise, you'll have to temporarily support the sink while you unfasten the mounting clips.

The easiest way to do this is with some wire and a couple of scraps of wood. Twist the wire around one piece, drop it down through the drain opening, wrap it around the other scrap, and tighten it like a tourniquet.

After removing the clips, support the sink with both hands, and have someone else slowly loosen the tourniquet until the sink pulls free.

Removing a toilet

It takes just a few minutes and a couple of wrenches to remove a toilet. Begin by shutting the stop and disconnecting the supply line from the stop and the tank. If your toilet doesn't have a stop, plan to install one before bringing in the new fixture.

Next, get as much water as you can out of the tank and bowl. Remove the tank cover and flush the toilet, holding the lever down to drain as much water as possible. Sponge out all the water that remains in the tank and bowl.

Two people can lift an entire toilet (but just barely), and toilets are really awkward to carry. That's why it's best to remove the tank first, then the bowl. (Of course, with a one-piece toilet you have no choice but to take out the whole thing at once.)

The tank rests on the back of the bowl, secured by a couple of bolts. Unfasten these and the tank will lift free.

With some older toilets, the tank is bolted to the wall and connected to the bowl with a chrome elbow. To remove this kind of tank, remove the elbow, then unbolt the tank from the wall.

Caps cover the bolts that hold the bowl to the floor. Pry these off and loosen the nuts. If a toilet's nuts and bolts are hopelessly corroded, saw or chisel them off. A wax ring seals the bottom of the bowl to a flange underneath. Before removing the bowl, rock it back and forth to break the seal.

Finally, scrape what remains of the wax ring off the floor and stuff a rag into the drain opening so gases can't back up.

1 *Shut off the stop*, *then loosen the nut that connects the supply line to the stop. To make the tank easier to maneuver, disconnect the supply line from the tank, too.*

2 *Remove the nuts from the tank hold-down bolts with a wrench. If they refuse to budge, squirt them with penetrating oil and/or try a bigger wrench.*

3 *To remove the tank you may need to rock it slightly to break it free. Next, remove the nuts that hold the bowl in place, rock it to break the wax seal underneath, and haul out the bowl.*

4 *Block sewer gas by stuffing a rag into the pipe. Sewer gas not only smells bad, it can explode. Set a bucket upside-down over the opening so debris won't fall in.*

Taking out a tub

The first task in removing a tub is getting access to the plumbing lines. If your tub has no access panel, cut an opening in the wall so you can get at the pipes.

Many older tubs lack shut-off valves. This means you'll have to cut and cap the supply lines. After that, loosen the slip nuts, and remove the drain, trap, and overflow tube. The way you remove the tub itself depends on what it's made of.

Steel and fiberglass tubs

Start by chipping away the wall materials around the edges of the tub to reveal the flange that secures the tub to the studs.

After removing the screws from the flange, tip the tub on its side, recruit a helper or two, and carry it out. Stand the tub on end to maneuver through tight spots.

Cast-iron tubs

A cast-iron bathtub weighs several hundred pounds, too much to easily lift and carry. The solution? A sledge hammer.

To keep the chips from flying, cover the tub with a drop cloth before attacking it. Cast-iron shards are incredibly sharp and need to be handled with extreme care during demolition and clean-up – they can cut through cloth gloves in a flash.

The network of pipes at the head of a tub includes a pipe that rises from the shower diverter to the showerhead. In the center, supply lines bring hot and cold water to the faucet assembly. Below, brass tubing drops from the tub overflow to a drain-trap assembly located beneath the tub. Dismantle these before demolishing or removing the tub.

Use a sledge hammer to demolish a cast-iron tub. Short, fast blows help minimize vibrations that can damage nearby plaster and drywall. Even so, you can expect to rattle nearby walls and any ceilings below.

1 *Unscrew supply lines* and cut off their fittings using a tubing cutter. Unscrew galvanized pipes.

2 *Cap supply lines* with caps made of the same material as the pipe. Galvanized caps are threaded. Attach plastic caps with special glue (see page 48).

3 *Solder on copper caps* after cleaning the pipe end and applying flux. (See page 49 for more about soldering joints.)

New life for old tubs

Think twice before taking a sledge to that old claw foot tub. The style is so popular that many manufacturers even offer reproduction models. If the tub just has to go, it might be worth the effort to get it out in one piece. There are many homeowners who would be happy to buy it.

2 *Break up the tile* and substrate with a fist maul. Don't try to smash everything to bits, just punch holes in the wall.

1 *To save the wall* above the tub surround, make a cut just above the top row of tile with a reciprocating saw. Avoid cutting the studs by holding the saw at a shallow angle so you cut only the drywall or plaster and lath.

Removing Ceramic Tile

Don't even bother trying to salvage ceramic tile. The tile itself comes off easily enough, but removing the grout and adhesive from the tile is almost impossible. Trying to salvage the underlayment is a lost cause, too. If you actually manage to get the tile off without damaging the underlayment, you'll undoubtedly wreck it when you try to remove the adhesive.

Instead, remove entire sections of tile and its backing, then replace the drywall or underlayment.

Wall tile

With a reciprocating saw, cut along a line at the top of the tile. Don't remove any more drywall or plaster and lath than you have to.

Now use a fist maul to bash up the tile and backing material. After you've fractured a wall section, tear it from the studs, tile and all. Finally, remove any nails or screws that remain in the studs.

Floor tile

First try chipping floor tile from the substrate with a fist maul and chisel. If this doesn't work, use a sledge hammer to bust up both the tile and the substrate.

If the substrate is underlayment, pull it up, too. If the tile was set on a mortar bed, removing it is a two-step process. The first round of the sledge-fest loosens the tiles from the mud bed, but often leaves the mortar mostly intact. After clearing out the tile,

3 *Grab sections* of tile and substrate and pull them free. The materials are heavy, so break up and remove small areas at a time.

you'll probably need a second round with the sledge (or a fist maul and cold chisel) to break up the mortar bed. Really tough cases may even require a jackhammer (which you can rent).

Shovel tile and concrete refuse into small containers and dump them before they get full – this stuff is heavy!

Oops!

Don't get carried away when swinging a fist maul, sledge hammer, or other weapon of destruction. Work slowly and carefully to protect yourself, your co-worker, and any materials or fixtures you plan on saving.

That's not a lesson you want to learn the hard way. On a previous Hometime remodeling project, a sledge hammer got out of hand (literally) and smashed a big hole in the wall of an adjacent bedroom.

Removing Resilient Flooring

If you know for sure that the resilient floor in your bathroom does not contain asbestos, feel free to tear it up. But first ask yourself if you really want to do this. Often it's better to just let an old floor lie and install a new one on top of it.

If the existing floor and its underlayment are in good shape (no sagging or bouncing, and no loose areas of flooring), you can install new underlayment and flooring over the old.

On the other hand, if the old floor is sagging or badly deteriorated, taking out the existing flooring may be necessary. Fortunately, it isn't very difficult to remove resilient flooring.

First see if you can get at the underlayment. If you can pry it up, flooring and all, in one or a few large chunks, you'll save time (and replacing underlayment is a minor cost). If that doesn't work, try these steps for removing tiles and sheet goods.

Resilient tiles

First use a heat gun or an old electric iron to soften several tiles. As the edges begin to curl, lift the tiles with a scraper. After you've removed these tiles, try taking up the others with a square-nose garden spade.

If you decide to reuse the underlayment, scrape off any remaining adhesive. Don't sand it – some old adhesives contain trace amounts of asbestos.

Sheet flooring

Begin by softening the edges and any seams with a heat gun or iron. Most bathroom floors will peel up in one or two sheets. If yours won't, use a utility knife to slice the flooring into strips and pull the strips free. Again, scrape away any remaining adhesive if you plan to reuse the underlayment.

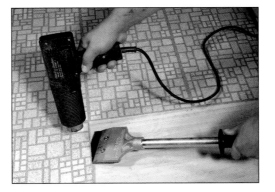

A heat gun makes vinyl tile easier to remove. Gently heat the edges of a couple tiles until the edges begin to lift, then pry up the tiles with a floor scraper or 6-inch taping knife.

Cut sheet goods in strips if it won't come up in one piece. Make cuts every 8 to 10 inches. If the paper backing sticks to the underlayment, lightly spray it with water, then scrape it up with a floor scraper.

New flooring over old

If the flooring in your bathroom flunks its asbestos test, you have three choices: a) pay big bucks to an asbestos abatement company and have them remove the floor; b) carefully remove the tiles and underlayment yourself, a tricky and potentially dangerous procedure; or c) lay a new floor over the old one, encasing the asbestos where it can't do any harm.

You'll probably opt for "c", which is the safest and least expensive way to go. You can lay any new flooring over any old material, except carpet. New resilient tiles and sheet goods can go directly over old, stable tiles, but in most cases, it's best to install ¼-inch plywood underlayment first. For a ceramic tile floor, you'll need to put down cement backer board.

Of course underlayment, plus the thickness of the new finish flooring, will raise your bathroom floor by half an inch or so. This presents both a tripping hazard and a wheelchair access issue. The simplest (but not necessarily the best) solution is to install a beveled threshold to ease the difference in floor heights to ¼ inch or less. This reduces the chance of tripping and provides bumpy access – but access nonetheless – for wheelchairs.

If the bathroom is regularly used by someone in a wheelchair, the better (and unfortunately, more expensive) solution is to have the existing floor removed and new flooring installed flush with the floor outside the bathroom.

Disconnecting Wiring

Electrical demolition moves along quickly. Your goal is to get every switch, receptacle, and light fixture out of harm's way. The only tools needed to accomplish this are a screwdriver, needle-nose pliers, and a neon

1 *To remove a switch*, *shut off power, remove the wall plate, back out screws through ears on the device, and gently pull it from the box.*

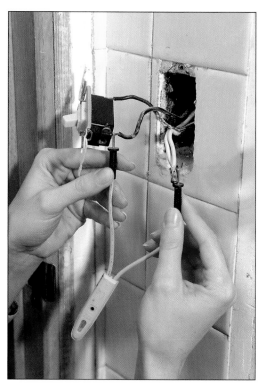

2 *A neon tester* *verifies that the power is off. Touch one of the probes to a hot terminal (brass screw) and the other to a neutral terminal (silver screw). If the tester lights, the circuit is still live.*

3 *Disconnect wires* *from the switch, join them with wire connectors, and neatly fold everything back into the box.*

tester – plus a handful of wire connectors to cap off the bare ends of wires.

Shut off the power

Begin by shutting off power at the breaker or fuse box and posting a sign warning others not to turn it back on again. Just to be sure, use a neon tester on each device, touching one probe to a hot (brass) terminal, the other to a neutral (silver) terminal. If the tester lights up, you're in for another trip to the service panel to find the right circuit.

Caution: Test your tester to make sure it works. Insert the probes into the slots of a receptacle you know is live. If the tester doesn't light up, throw it away and buy a new one.

Disconnecting fixtures

When the tester doesn't light up, unscrew the wires from the device, straighten them out with the pliers, and twist on wire connectors, joining hot to hot wires, neutral to neutral.

Generally, hot wires are black and neutrals white but there are exceptions. If you run across red wires, they are usually hot. Also, an older house may have only black wires or someone may have wired a 3-way switch and neglected to code the white wire to show that it's hot. If you have any doubts about which wires are hot and which are neutral, call an electrician. CAUTION: If you find wires in a fixture, switch, or receptacle box that don't seem to have anything to do with the device, leave them alone. They're probably going elsewhere in your house.

Finally, neatly tuck the wires and connectors back into the box where they can't be accidentally damaged. When there are several switches in one box, it's a good idea to label the pairs of wires ("light" and "fan," for example) so you can correctly hook everything up again.

Let it hang

If you're planning to hire an electrician to run new wiring, don't go overboard in dismantling the old wiring. Electrical contractors often say, "Let it hang." It's a lot easier to see what's what if all the old wiring remains in place. Neatly coil cables to get them out of the way.

Disconnecting Plumbing

Compared with electrical demolition, dismantling plumbing lines is hard, noisy work – especially if you have to contend with old-fashioned galvanized pipe. Galvanized pipe hasn't been used in years, but there's still plenty of it out there, and if yours is an older home, it will probably have some back behind the walls.

As you may recall, codes generally allow you to move the lavatory about three feet. Doing this will mean rerouting the drain line and the vertical vent that lets the drain breathe. Of course, you'll have to take out some of the old pipes first – a good job for that trusty demolition tool, the reciprocating saw.

Because the old pipes were threaded together in order, one into another, you can't just take a wrench and break into a run at any point that's convenient for you. Instead, make at least two cuts, remove the section between them, then work with wrenches backward and forward from the break.

This is where the reciprocating saw comes in. Fitted with a metal-cutting blade, it makes short work of copper and plastic pipes. It also offers the best way to cut galvanized pipes, although the going is slower and noisier.

After cutting into a run, you need to unthread the sections you don't want, a job that sounds easier than it usually is. The problem is that corrosion practically welds old pipe joints together. Breaking them loose calls for lots of muscle. Squirting the joints with penetrating oil and/or banging them with a hammer sometimes helps.

To remove galvanized pipes, make two cuts, about three inches apart, in the run you want to remove. Here, we've reversed the saw blade for better access. Wear hearing protection – this saw is loud.

Use a pipe wrench to turn pipes loose from fittings. If a joint is stuck tight, spray it with penetrating oil or give it some friendly persuasion with a hammer. Here the T-fitting has already been removed, and the drain has been plugged with a rag.

Reciprocating saw safety

With the proper blade, a reciprocating saw takes all sorts of demolition jobs in stride – pipes, studs, drywall, plaster, lath, plywood, insulation, even tree branches. But like any tool, especially a workhorse as powerful as this one, a reciprocating saw deserves respect.

First, keep in mind that a reciprocating saw is a two-handed tool. Because it has a great tendency to vibrate and kick back when cutting, get a firm grip, and always hold the shoe firmly against the work.

With a variable-speed saw or a two-speed saw, cut metal at low speed, wood at high speed. Before cutting into a wall, floor, ceiling, or other surface, check for hidden pipes or wires. If you're not sure what's in there, make a series of shallow cuts until you can evaluate the situation.

When you change blades, make sure the blade is fully seated before tightening the screw. Finally, as with any power tool, always unplug a reciprocating saw when you're changing blades or not using it.

Removing Walls

Start the demolition by cutting small openings between studs. Peer inside. Pipes, wiring, and ducts will have to be relocated. Don't assume that any wiring you see is on the same circuit as the bathroom. If there are wires that aren't serving outlets in the wall, shut off all power at the service panel until you determine where the wires are going.

Remove surface materials

To remove drywall, punch a series of holes through the drywall in the middle of a stud cavity. Then grab hold of the jagged edges of the drywall and pull to break off large pieces; use the hooked end of a crowbar to lever stubborn pieces.

Cut studs with a reciprocating saw. Cut each one in the middle, then pry the ends free from the sole and top plates.

Pry off plates with a crowbar. Starting at one end, work the crowbar's claw underneath the plate and lift it an inch or so, then work your way along the plate until it comes free.

With plaster, follow a three-step process: break a chunk loose with a crowbar, pull the plaster from the lath, then pry the lath from the studs. Keep a trash can nearby for the debris. Empty the can before it's full or it'll be too heavy to lift.

Finally, pull out any nails and screws left in the studs.

Take out the studs

After you've exposed the framing, reroute any wiring in the wall. Then cut each stud using a reciprocating saw with a bi-metal blade. After each cut, pull the pieces free from the top and sole plates. Don't batter the studs – you could crack plaster or drywall on the ceiling or adjoining walls.

Pry the end studs loose, using scraps of lumber under the crowbar to avoid marring the walls. Framing lumber can be reused, but first remove all nails and saw off split ends.

Pry off the plates

Carefully pry the sole and top plates from the floor and ceiling. Lever against a scrap so you don't damage the ceiling or floor. (This also gives more leverage for pulling those long nails.)

Point of no return. Your bathroom will look pretty grungy at this point, but keep in mind, it will all be worth it in the end.

ROUGH-INS

Contractors and building inspectors *call the framing, pipes, wires, and ducts that make up your home's infrastructure rough work, and they call the process of installing them roughing in. With rough-ins, appearances don't matter – after all, everything will be covered up with wallboard later on.*

But rough doesn't mean sloppy. Framing must come out level, plumb, square, and structurally sound. Plumbing calls for careful measurements, leak-free connections, and waste lines that drain properly. Wiring must be installed in ways that protect against shock and fire. And most important of all, laws and common sense dictate that all rough work be done to code.

Framing

A simple expansion (such as a partition wall with a door opening) calls for only very basic carpentry, and should take just a few hours. Of course, if you plan to remodel within the confines of an existing bathroom, you might not need to do any framing at all.

Installing plates

Every partition begins with 2x4 plates nailed to the floor and ceiling. Cut them to length, lay them side by side on the floor, then mark the points on each plate where the studs will be nailed. Space these markings 16 inches apart, center to center (also called on center).

Position the sole plate (also called a bottom plate) and drive 12-penny nails through the sole plate into the subfloor. If possible, nail the top plate to rafters, joists, or nailers above the ceiling. Otherwise, secure the top plate with construction adhesive and nail the end studs into the sidewall framing.

Mark stud locations with Xs that indicate which side of the line the stud goes on. Space the studs 16 inches on center.

When toenailing studs, drive the first nail near the edge of the stud. Pound the next nail through the middle of the opposite side. Then it's back to side one for the third nail.

Toenailing studs

Now measure the distance between each set of marks on the plates and cut studs to fit. Don't assume that the lengths will all be exactly equal because floors and ceilings aren't always perfectly level.

Tap each stud into position between the marks and use a level to be sure it's plumb in both directions. Toenail the studs by driving nails at an angle through their sides into the plate.

To do this, brace the stud with your foot and drive a nail into one side, close to the edge. Don't worry if the stud moves slightly, because when you drive a second nail through the other side – in the center this time – the stud will slide back into position. Finally, drive a third nail through the first side near the other edge.

Header   Top plate   Stud

Jack stud   King stud   Sole plate

All partition walls have the same framing elements, regardless of their length and height. A top plate and sole plate anchor the wall to the ceiling and floor. If possible, also anchor the partition to the sidewalls.

The edges of vertical studs, spaced 16 inches on center, provide nailing surfaces for drywall. These are toenailed in place.

Beefed up framing around a door opening supports the hinges and latch. Jack studs at the sides support a header up top.

Framing a door opening

To determine the size of the rough opening, measure the door and add 2 inches to its width and 2 inches to its height above the level of the finished flooring you'll be installing.

Install the studs to either side of the opening. Then nail a shorter 2x4 jack stud to each side of the opening. These support a header at the top of the opening. A header in a partition wall typically consists of two 2x4s, one on top of the other. With a wider opening, or if the ceiling is more than a few inches higher than the door, you'll need a short cripple stud between the header and the top plate.

A pedestal sink bolts to the wall, which means you'll need blocking there. Later, when the sink is installed, its mounting bracket will be secured to the blocking.

Install blocking to provide rock-solid anchors for any grab bars you might install later. Blocking is just 2x8s cut to fit between studs and nailed in place. Grab bars cannot be anchored to studs alone, so a few minutes of work now could save a lot of time and money down the road.

Installing a replacement window

Moisture takes its toll on wood bathroom windows. If yours is rotting and leaking air, you'll be energy dollars ahead to replace it with a new fiberglass unit.

Sometimes you can find a replacement window that exactly fits the rough opening for the old one. It's more likely, though, that you'll have to reduce or enlarge the existing opening.

The rough opening is generally about 1 inch wider and ½ inch taller than the window. The header is 3 inches wider than the new window's rough opening. The jack studs fit under the header, while the king studs extend up to the top plate.

After cutting back the sheathing to expose the new opening, set the new window in place and shim it level and plumb.

Secure the window by driving roofing nails through the nailing flange around the exterior. Reinstall any exterior trim and replace the siding.

Framing a tub deck

The walls that support a tub deck are framed just like regular walls – top and bottom plates with studs running 16 inches on center between them. If the tub is light enough for a few people to lift into place, go ahead and frame the entire deck. For an exceptionally large and/or heavy tub, frame the back half of the deck, slide the tub in place, then frame the front portion of the deck around the tub.

When figuring the height of the tub deck, remember to account for a sheet of ¾ inch exterior-grade plywood, plus another inch for cement backer board, mortar, and ceramic tile.

Frame the tub deck with 2x4 lumber, making sure to leave a framed opening for the access panel. Secure the frame to the wall studs and floor joists with construction adhesive and drywall screws. Install angled corner braces positioned to support the tub corners.

Use exterior-grade plywood for the tub deck. Size the opening using the template that came with the tub. Drill a starter hole with a ¼-inch bit, then cut out the opening with a jig saw. (If the opening has straight sides, it'll be easier to make the straight cuts with a circular saw, then switch to the jig saw for any curved cuts.)

Framing a shower stall

If you can frame a wall, you can frame a shower stall. If you are using a prefabricated shower pan, its dimensions determine the width and depth of the stall.

Walls for a shower stall consist of 2x4 plates and studs. In addition, you must install blocking between the stud bottoms for fastening the shower pan, 1x4 bracing in the plumbing wall to support the top of the shower riser and the faucet valve, and nailers in the corners for backer board if the stall will be tiled.

Frame the wall on the floor if the floor and ceiling are reasonably level. Otherwise, fasten the plates, then measure, cut, and nail in the studs one at a time, a process called stick-building. On the plumbing wall, space the studs to accommodate the pipes and shower fittings.

To accommodate drain and vent pipes in a plumbing wall, notch the sole plate, slide the wall into place, then bridge the gaps in the plate with steel protector plates.

Fasten the sole plate to the floor joist with construction adhesive and drywall screws. With slab construction or a basement bathroom, drive masonry nails with a powder-actuated nailer.

Fasten the end stud to a wall stud, or to blocking installed between the wall studs if the shower wall doesn't line up with an existing wall stud.

Plumbing

Plumbing relies on two simple physical principles: pressure brings water to fixtures and gravity carries it away. The pressure side of the system consists of hot and cold water supply pipes; the gravity side includes DWV (short for drain/waste/vent) pipes. Some parts of each system can easily be modified, others can't – the trick is to know the difference.

Supply pipes

The supply system starts at the meter and shutoff valve with a single line to the water heater. From there, the system branches into separate networks for hot and cold water. These run parallel to fixtures throughout your home.

Because they're relatively small in diameter (typically about ¾ inch) and under 50 to 60 pounds of pressure, supply lines can go almost anywhere – rerouting them is no big deal. You can bore holes to route them through studs, run pipes vertically through floors and the cavities between studs, and turn 90-degree corners.

DWV pipes

Drain/waste/vent pipes are an entirely different story. With these, a vertical stack (your home may have more than one) serves as the system's trunk. The stack rises from a sewer line at its base and climbs up through the roof. Drain pipes from fixtures empty into the stack. Each fixture also connects to vertical and horizontal vent pipes that release gases into the stack, where they rise through the roof and dissipate in outdoor air. More important, venting prevents draining waste water from sucking the water out of traps, which would let sewer gases seep into your home.

DWV pipes are much bigger in diameter than supply lines, and because they rely on gravity, drain lines must slope ¼ inch per foot according to most codes. Anything beyond minor modification to a DWV system requires costly plumbing work, and often a lot of carpentry to cover up relocated pipes.

Supply pipes, indicated in red and blue, bring hot and cold water to fixtures. DWV pipes, shown here in white, carry away waste water and equalize air pressure in the system. Start the rough-in work with the DWV system. It's easier to install these larger pipes before you run the smaller-diameter supply lines.

Pipes and fittings

Pipes and fittings come in a variety of materials, including galvanized steel, copper, plastic, cast iron, and brass. The one you choose depends partly on the job you want it to do and partly on the materials permitted by local codes.

Galvanized pipes carry both fresh and waste water. Because it's hard to work with, tends to lime up, and eventually rusts out, galvanized isn't widely used these days.

Supply fittings include Ts, 90- and 45-degree elbows, couplings, caps, and reducers. Copper and plastic fittings aren't threaded; galvanized fittings are. Any run of galvanized pipe also includes a union fitting somewhere. It compensates for the fact that all pipes have right-hand threads by letting you thread pipes into fittings at either end of a run.

Copper

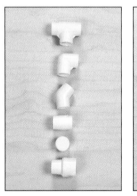

CPVC

Galvanized steel

DWV fittings are bigger than supply fittings. Among them are sanitary T's, sweeping elbows, sanitary elbows, 45-degree elbows, couplings, adapters, and trap assemblies. Note that there are two kinds of elbows. Drain fittings have eased angles so waste doesn't get caught in the fitting, vent fittings make a sharper turn.

PVC

ABS

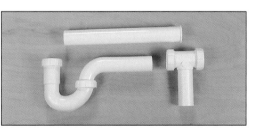

Trap assembly

Copper pipes serve as supply lines and are sometimes used in DWV runs as well. They're lightweight, highly durable, and allowed by virtually all codes.

Plastic pipes are now widely used in DWV systems, and some codes also permit them for supply lines. To keep things simple, plastic pipes are known by the abbreviations for their different chemical makeups. PVC is used for DWV lines and cold water supply lines; CPVC is used for both hot and cold supply lines; ABS is used for DWV lines only. Don't mix different kinds of plastic pipe in the same run; they expand at different rates.

Cast iron is strictly for drain lines. Old-fashioned hub and spigot joints were packed with oakum, then sealed with molten lead. Today, no-hub fittings make cast iron easier to work with, and also let you join different DWV pipe materials. Cast-iron drain lines are considerably quieter than plastic drain lines.

Brass pipes serve as supply lines in a few older homes, but today brass is used mainly for drain fittings such as traps and tub overflows (items that are also available in plastic).

Use transition fittings to join different pipe materials – extending a new PVC drainline from an existing galvanized line, for example. Dielectric fittings separate different pipe materials, such as galvanized and copper or brass, that corrode when they come in contact with each other.

Where you'll find lead and asbestos

Joints soldered before 1988 could contain lead-based solder. Tying new copper into old rattles joints down the line and could knock loose bits of solder. Lead-based or not, you need to flush the particles out of the system.

To clear particles from supply pipes, remove all faucet aerators and thoroughly flush the lines after you turn the water back on.

If you encounter asbestos insulation on pipes, leave it alone. If you need to cut into a pipe that's asbestos wrapped – or if any of the asbestos insulation is deteriorating – it's time to call in a pro. Taking out old asbestos pipe insulation is a job for a certified asbestos abatement contractor. Call your local health board or EPA office for a list of approved contractors.

Moving a sink

Plumbing codes require that every fixture be properly vented. Otherwise, a vacuum in the drainage system could pull water out of a trap and let sewer gas into the house.

Does this mean that every fixture must empty directly into a vented drain line? Not always. Most plumbing codes give you some leeway with certain fixtures, such as a sink. This means you can legally move a sink a few feet to one side or another of an existing DWV connection. Under most codes, you can even drain a second sink into the extended drain line.

Extending drain lines

You can move a sink as far as you can extend its drain pipe; the length of the new drain pipe is determined by its diameter. Typically you can extend a 1½-inch PVC drain up to 42 inches, so you could move the sink that distance and remain in compliance with code.

Your first task is to install a new plastic sanitary T in the old DWV line. PVC pipe is easy stuff to work with. You cut it with a hack saw and glue the pipe and fittings together. To connect PVC to galvanized pipe, use a transition fitting.

After substituting a couple lengths of PVC and the sanitary T for the section of pipe that was removed, route another length of PVC through the studs. This entails boring holes through the studs with a hole saw and right-angle drill. Here again, codes specify how big the holes can be. A threaded elbow that the trap assembly will screw into completes the installation.

Extending supply lines

With the DWV work out of the way, you can turn to the supply lines. Copper tubing requires smaller holes than drain pipes, and sweat-soldering the connections is easy, once you know how. With plastic supply lines, keep expansion in mind. Bore oversize holes, otherwise the pipes will creak, groan, and maybe even leak.

Finally, to protect against piercing the copper and plastic lines with nails or screws when you put up the drywall, install metal plates on the edges of the studs.

To move a sink, you must extend the drain and supply lines. New PVC pipe and a sanitary T tie into the old DWV pipe. A sloping lateral pipe and elbow complete the new drain installation.

Use a right-angle drill to make holes slightly larger than the pipe. Plan the pipe run so the drain line slopes ¼ inch per foot toward the sanitary T.

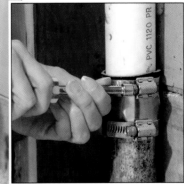

A transition fitting joins PVC to galvanized pipes. Slip the neoprene sleeve and clamps onto one of the pipes, butt the pipes, position the sleeve, then tighten the clamps.

Cut plastic pipe with a hacksaw or a power miter saw. Measure carefully; pipe fittings provide no margin for error. Cut, preassemble, and check all pipe runs before gluing or soldering them.

Gluing PVC pipe

Gluing, or solvent welding, plastic pipe is much easier than sweating copper, but that's not a license to be sloppy. There are procedures you must follow in order to make leak-free joints.

Measure pipe lengths carefully – remember to account for the portions of the pipe that fit inside the fittings. If possible, cut the pipe with a miter box or power miter saw. A square-cut end will seat fully against the shoulder of the fitting and will be less likely to leak.

Test-fit all the pieces before gluing them together. Don't force the pipe ends into the fittings, you may not be able to pull them apart again. When it's time to glue the joint, the cement will act as a lubricant, allowing the pipe to seat properly in the fitting. Do tip up the pipe and check that the fitting isn't loose enough to slip off on its own. If it does, get a different fitting. Joints that are too loose or too tight won't weld together.

Plastic pipe is more flexible than metal pipe. Be sure to support horizontal runs with plastic pipe hangers anywhere the pipe is not supported by the framing. Space hangers every 3 to 4 feet (or as required by local code).

1 *Scrape all burrs* from the cut end with a knife or file. Burrs can scrape away cement and weaken the bond.

2 *Gluing PVC* is a two-step process. First brush on a purple primer, then a clear solvent. Primer softens the plastic, allowing the solvent cement to weld the pieces together. Use glue and primer made specifically for the plastic you are using or else use a universal solvent.

3 *Coat the inside* of the socket and the outside of the pipe end with primer. The color makes it easy to see if you've missed any spots. Use primer with PVC and CPVC pipe, but not with ABS, which has its own self-priming solvent.

4 *Spread an even coating* of solvent cement onto the pipe end, then into the fitting socket. Don't let cement puddle in the fitting. To keep the solvent cement from thickening, cap it until you're ready to make the next joint.

5 *Push the pipe* all the way into the fitting, then give it a quarter turn. Hold the pipe in place for 10 seconds so the pipe doesn't pull out of the tapered fitting. If you used enough cement, you'll see a small bead of glue around the joint.

Sweating copper joints

Sweating a joint can be intimidating the first time you try it. But with just a little practice, you'll soon have the hang of it.

If the solder won't melt, the problem could be water in the pipe. Pipes that aren't absolutely dry won't heat up enough to melt solder. If all efforts to drain the pipe fail, stuff a piece of bread (use white bread with the crust cut off) in the pipe end. It will stop the moisture and eventually disintegrate.

When the joint has cooled a bit, wipe it off with a wet rag. This makes a neat looking joint, plus it removes excess flux that would eventually corrode the copper.

1 *Cut copper pipe* with a tubing cutter. Use the cutter's pointed reamer to cut away burrs inside the pipe.

2 *Polish the pipe end* with emery cloth (don't use steel wool, it will leave fibers on the pipe). Solder and flux adhere best to a clean surface. Don't touch polished surfaces – a fingerprint could impede the flow of solder.

3 *Clean inside the fitting* with a wire brush. Remove all grease, dirt, and oxidation – flux will not adhere to a dirty surface.

4 *Apply a coat* of flux to the outside of the pipe end and the inside of the fitting. Join the pipe and fitting and gently twist them back and forth to evenly spread the flux.

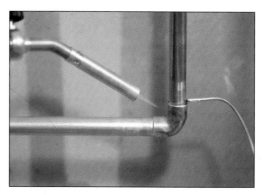

5 *Move the torch* back and forth to avoid burning off the flux. Heat only the fitting, never the pipe. Touch solder to the side of the joint opposite the flame. Once the solder starts to melt, pull the flame away from the fitting. There's no need to move the solder around the joint. Capillary action will draw the solder into and around the joint.

Pipes rise from the stop valves to the faucet valve. Pipes from the faucet valve connect to elbow fittings onto which you will later thread the spout and showerhead.

Blocking between the studs supports the showerhead, faucet, and spout connections. A notch in the faucet blocking accommodates the shower riser.

Under the floor, a new PVC elbow is connected to the existing galvanized drain pipe with a transition fitting.

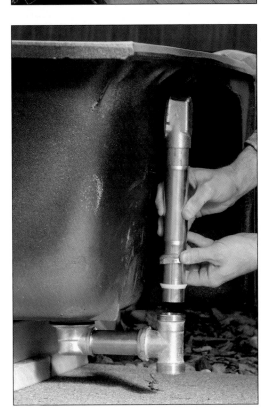

A pipe with a slip fitting goes from the overflow into a T fitting. Under the tub, the drain assembly also connects to the threaded T fitting.

Tub and shower rough-in

While the other plumbing fixtures don't get installed until the end of the project, a tub has to be installed now, in the rough-in phase, before the walls are closed up and tiled. First you have to rough-in plumbing hookups for the faucet and showerhead.

Insulate

Now's the time to insulate and attach vapor barriers to the walls around the tub area. You won't be able to get at the lower parts of those walls after the tub is in place. On exterior walls, cut the batts to length with a utility knife, loosely fit them into stud cavities, then fasten a polyethylene vapor barrier to the framing with a hammer stapler.

It's also a good idea to insulate interior walls for soundproofing. Tuck insulation around the tub, too. It'll keep bathwater warmer for longer periods of time if you do.

Installing the tub drain and overflow

It's easiest to do this before the tub goes into place. First prop up the tub with 2x4s so you can get at the drain opening. Now lay a bead of plumber's putty around the drain and overflow openings. Fit the drain body with a rubber gasket, push it up through the opening, and screw the strainer into it. Then connect the overflow tube to the drain T with a slip nut.

Be careful that you don't overtighten drain fittings – it's easy to crack relatively soft brass or plastic. Always hand-tighten the fittings first, then go an extra quarter turn with pliers or a wrench.

Finally, install the pop-up or trip-lever assembly that closes the drain. Follow the instructions that came with it; procedures vary from one manufacturer to another.

Setting a cast-iron tub

Begin by installing a 2x4 ledger along the back wall. The tub flange will rest on this; the tub itself will rest on the subfloor.

It takes more than two people to carry in a cast-iron tub. Lay 2x4 runners in the tub enclosure, shove the tub into place on top of the ledger, then slowly pull out the runners. Check to be sure the tub is level. If it's not, pull the tub back out and adjust the ledger.

After the tub is solidly in place, connect the drain assembly to the drain line with a trap. Because the trap drops below the floor,

Install insulation and a vapor barrier before the tub goes in. Always wear protective clothing when working with insulation; fiberglass fibers can irritate your eyes, respiratory tract, and skin.

you'll find yourself working in tight quarters down there. You may need to cut away some subflooring to gain access.

Finishing touches – the spout, showerhead, and faucet handles – are installed after the walls are tiled.

Setting a steel or fiberglass tub

Two people can maneuver a lightweight steel or fiberglass tub. After the tub is in place, drive screws through holes in the flanges into the wall studs. Otherwise, installation procedures are the same as for the cast-iron tub.

Cover your new tub with drop cloths to protect it from construction debris and the inevitable dropped tool.

Roughing in a shower stall

Plumbing hookups for a stand-alone shower are the same as those for a tub/shower combination, minus the spout and diverter, of course. Locate the faucets 38 to 48 inches above floor level. Set the showerhead at no lower than 66 inches, but feel free to raise this height for comfort.

Make the drain connection and set the shower base before closing up the walls. If your plan calls for a manufactured stall, set it now, too. A prefab shower stall or glass door assembly may require additional studs and blocking for rigidity. Follow the manufacturer's specifications.

As with a tub, installing insulation and a vapor barrier around a shower stall deadens sound and prevents moisture problems in adjoining rooms.

You'll need help tipping and shoving a cast-iron tub into position. Slide it along 2x4 skids. Have one person use another 2x4 to keep the drain assembly clear of the subflooring.

A 2x4 ledger supports the back of the tub. The weight of a cast-iron tub holds it in place; steel and fiberglass tubs must be screwed to framing members.

Whirlpool Tubs

When to install a whirlpool tub depends on the type of tub and what works best for you. A standard-sized alcove tub goes in during rough-in, but a deck-mounted tub should be installed after the tub deck is finished – if the tub can fit through the door. Otherwise, you'll have to juggle the usual construction order so you finish the tub deck and install the tub, then move on to finish the rest of the bathroom.

Tub installation

Before installing the tub, attach the drain assembly and inspect all the factory-installed pipes and hoses for loose connections. Then, round up some helpers – even lightweight acrylic whirlpool tubs weigh over 100 pounds, and maneuvering them over a deck can be a back-wrenching experience. Set the tub in place, check it for level, and shim as needed.

Hookups

Once the tub is in place, make your plumbing hookups. Connect the drain assembly to the trap assembly and install the faucet, spout, and sprayer.

Most whirlpool tubs require a dedicated 20-amp circuit with a GFCI (ground-fault circuit interrupter) breaker. You can run the cable yourself, but have an electrician install the GFCI breaker. Before you make the electrical connections to the pump motor, make sure the power is off. Then connect wires from the power supply cable to the motor according to manufacturer's directions. Run a number-6 grounding wire from the motor to a copper cold-water supply line, using a ground clamp to make the connection to the pipe. If you're unsure of how to make the connections, have the electrician do the tub hookups, too.

Now, give the tub a test-run. Turn on the power and test the GFCI breaker. Fill the tub until the water is a few inches above the jets. Turn on the pump and check for leaks. Let the motor run for 20 minutes, just to make sure everything's working right.

Finally, place insulation around the tub – but not close to the pump or heater – before finishing the deck sides.

A tub this size weighs considerably more than a standard five-foot tub. Ask the dealer how much the tub you selected weighs when filled with water, then add the weight of the bathers. You may need to reinforce the joists if your new tub is bigger than the old one. Check with your building department to be sure.

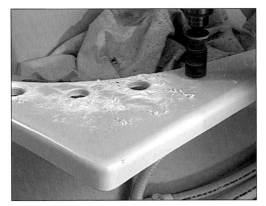

If the whirlpool isn't predrilled for a faucet, place the faucet where it's easily reached. Usually, that's the tub deck, but sometimes the tub rim works better. Use a hole saw to cut holes in an acrylic tub.

Prepare the base, if one is required. Some tubs sit on built-in feet, others rest on wood blocks or a mortar bed. Check the manufacturer's directions to see what your tub requires.

Wiring Rough-In

Before beginning the electrical rough-in, learn what your local code says about the materials you can use. Most call for 14-gauge Type NM (nonmetallic-sheathed) cable, and many allow plastic boxes; a few communities require metal boxes and armored cable or metal conduit.

Is a new circuit required?

In most cases the answer is no; if you're just adding a few new lights and maybe a ventilator, the original bathroom circuit should be adequate.

You will, however, need a separate circuit for the motor in a whirlpool tub. Extending an existing circuit is a fairly simple job, but running a new one could be tricky. Consider hiring an electrician for this, especially for making the final connection at the service panel (code in some areas requires an electrician to do this).

Running cable

Running cable through exposed studs is easy. Just nail boxes to the studs, bore holes through the studs, and run cable to the boxes. Maneuvering cables through covered stud and joist cavities is trickier. With these you'll need to fish the cables.

GFCI

The letters stand for ground-fault circuit interrupter, and virtually all of today's electrical codes require them in bathrooms and other wet locations.

Why? Because even though modern-day electrical systems are grounded with a third conductor that protects against a serious shock, electricity can leak from the hot conductor without tripping a circuit breaker.

If this occurs and you happen to be especially well-grounded (turning off a faucet while turning on a defective hair dryer, for example), then that leaked current would pass through your body on its way to the earth. The result could be fatal.

A GFCI device compares current levels in the hot and neutral sides of a circuit. These should always be equal. If the GFCI senses a difference of just $1/2000$ of an amp, it trips the circuit in $1/40$ of a second or less – quickly enough to prevent injury.

A GFCI receptacle *has two sets of terminals – one labeled load, the other, line. Wires coming in from the service panel connect to the line terminals.*

Connect outgoing wires to the load terminals. This provides GFCI protection to all the outlets that follow in the circuit.

Attach a grounding wire to the green grounding screw at the bottom of the device.

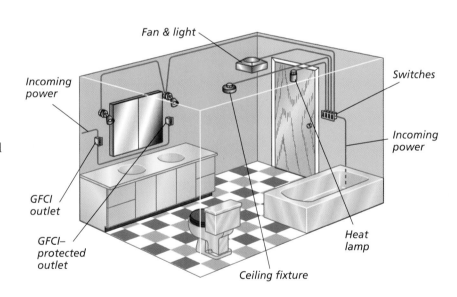

This electrical rough-in *is typical. It adds boxes for a few receptacles, wall and ceiling lights, and a combination ventilator/light. Everything (except the receptacles) will be controlled by a bank of four switches to the right of the door.*

Power for the bathroom circuit comes into the switch box, which will serve as a jumping-off point for cables to the receptacles, lights, and vent. The GFCI outlets tap power from another circuit.

Locating outlets

Codes specify where you can put switches and receptacles. Switches usually go 48 to 50 inches above the floor. Locate them to the latch side of the door. Just inside the bathroom is best, but if space is tight you can mount a switch (or switches) just outside.

You'll need at least one GFCI-protected receptacle near the sink, and with all of today's grooming appliances, two is even better. But this doesn't mean you need two GFCI devices. An ordinary receptacle connected to a GFCI receptacle offers GFCI protection. Most bathrooms don't need more than two receptacles, but if yours is a large one, locate additional outlets 12 to 16 inches above the floor, no more than 12 feet apart.

1 *Nail boxes* to the sides of studs. Most boxes have markings on them so that the box edge will end up flush with the wall surface you'll be installing.

2 *Use an angle drill* and a 7/8- or 1-inch bit to bore holes through framing. Drill at the center of each member.

3 *Feed cable* through the holes. On vertical runs, secure the cable with staples every 4½ feet, near changes in direction, and within 6 to 12 inches of boxes, depending on local code. Leave at least 8 inches of extra cable at each box for making connections.

Go fish

If you aren't opening up the walls, the way to run cable for new fixtures or circuits is with a fish tape. You may have to make small openings in the wall, ceiling, and/or floor in order to get the fish tape where it needs to go.

Feed the fish tape through the wall or ceiling until the tape emerges. Hook the cable to the fish tape and wrap the joint with electrical tape so the cable doesn't come loose.

Slowly reel in the fish tape and cable. If the cable gets caught, feed out some of the fish tape, have someone pull gently on the cable, and try again.

Installing a vent fan

Most codes specify a power ventilator only if your bathroom doesn't have a window. Even if your bathroom does have a window, you should install a vent fan – it's faster and more efficient at removing moisture.

Fans are sized according to the number of cubic feet of air they can move per minute (CFM), and codes typically require eight air changes per hour. However, there's no law that says you can't change air faster than eight times per hour, and often it costs only a few dollars to jump up a fan size. To compute the minimum fan capacity you need, divide the bathroom's size in cubic feet by 7.5.

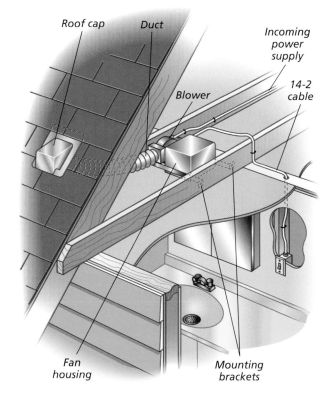

The blower and fan housing mount in the ceiling between joists. From there an insulated duct expels air to the outside through a roof cap. If your fan includes a light, run three-conductor cable to a pair of wall switches.

Look for the ratings label on any fan you're considering. It tells how much air the unit moves (CFM) and how much noise it makes (sones).

Fans also differ in the amount of noise they make, indicated by a sone rating. The lower the rating, the quieter the fan. (A 1.5-sone vent is only half as loud as a 3-sone model.)

Bathroom fans can vent through the roof or through an outside wall. Don't exhaust one into an attic, though; humidity from your bathroom will wreck the insulation. Instead, run a flexible insulated duct from the top of the ventilator to a roof cap or wall vent. The insulated duct assures that warm, moist air from the bathroom doesn't encounter cooler attic air, causing condensation in the duct that could drip back into the bathroom.

Venting through the roof calls for cutting a hole in the roofing and roof deck. If you're nervous about doing this – or have qualms about even climbing up there – hire a carpenter or roofer to do that part of the job.

Remove several shingles and cut a hole for the roof cap. After you install the cap, reinstall the shingles so that they cover the up-roof part of the cap's flashing. The lower part of the flashing should overlap shingles on the down-roof side.

After the roof cap is in place, cut a hole in the bathroom ceiling, connect the cable from the switches to wires in the vent unit's housing, install the housing in the ceiling opening, and connect the duct to the fan and the roof cap.

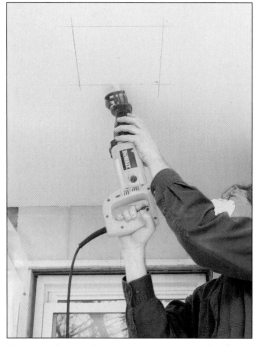

Use a reciprocating saw to cut an opening for the fan housing. Start the cut at a hole bored in one corner of the outline.

The framing inspector checks to make sure that holes bored for pipe runs won't weaken the studs. Codes specify how much wood must remain.

Inspection time

Now, with the rough-in completed but the walls still open, it's time to call the local building department and arrange for inspections of your structural, plumbing, and electrical work. In some communities this requires visits from three different inspectors; in other localities – especially for a project as contained as a bathroom remodeling – a single inspector might sign off on two or even all three rough-in elements.

If you've carefully adhered to codes, these inspections will be a formality, but an important one.

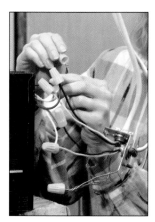

Make final connections according to the schematic that comes with the fan. Wrap stranded wires around solid wires in a clockwise direction.

Listen carefully to any suggestions an inspector might make. Inspectors see a lot of construction and they can be very helpful.

WALLS and CEILINGS

Drywall and its cousin, cement backer board, *are engineered building materials that have just about replaced old-fashioned plaster walls and ceilings. Install drywall in dry locations; use backer board as a base for ceramic tile or a fiberglass tub surround. Even if intact surfaces of your bathroom are plaster, piece in drywall or backer board to cover any openings. After you've taped and mudded the seams, and covered everything with paint, tile, or wallcovering, few people will ever notice the difference.*

Prep Work

Your finished surfaces will only be as good as what's underneath, so take time at the beginning of a drywall or backer board installation to survey your framing situation. All stud edges must align on the same plane, which means you may have to shim them out with wood, hardboard, or felt furring strips. If you're replacing part of a plaster wall with drywall, you'll have to fur out the studs to make the drywall flush with the plaster next to it.

You'll also need to plan the layout so that all panel edges will be supported by framing members. Make sure the layout uses as many full sheets as possible; this reduces the number of seams you'll have to fill and sand.

Install nailers

To give drywall and backer board panel edges proper support, you may need to install a few nailers. Scrap 2x4s nailed to the sides of studs and flush with their front edges work fine. Here again, appearances don't matter; the only purpose of a nailer is to provide solid lumber you can drive nails or screws into.

Protective nailing plates ensure that you won't puncture plumbing or electrical lines when hanging the drywall. Barbs at the top and bottom bite into the stud.

Don't skimp on insulation. Just a few dollars invested in materials will pay back big bucks on your heating and cooling bills.

Install a vapor barrier to protect studs and insulation from humidity. Use a hammer stapler to make short work of attaching a polyethylene vapor barrier to stud edges.

Plug energy leaks where plumbing or electrical lines pass from heated to unheated spaces (through a ceiling into the attic, for example). To keep air from escaping around the lines, fill the openings with insulating foam.

Finish insulating

Insulate as you go, first filling points where new framing will meet old, then, before installing the tub, fill the niche it fits into. Finally, insulate and install vapor barriers on any open exterior walls. Use as few staples as possible when installing a vapor barrier – each hole lessens its efficiency.

Install nailers anywhere they're needed to support the edges of drywall and backer board panels. You may need nailers on the studs adjacent to the tub edge. Drywall will meet the tub and backer board at this point.

Drywall

Until it's installed, drywall can be easily damaged. Corners are especially easy to wreck, so handle the sheets with care. Drywall is also a lot heavier than it looks. A 4x8 sheet of ½-inch-thick drywall weighs about 55 pounds, and carrying one is a job best managed by two people.

Cutting

Make straight cuts with a utility knife and a drywall T-square or a long straightedge. To do this, stand the panel on edge and lean it against the wall with its light-colored side toward you. Position the T-square edge on the cutting line and draw the knife along it, slicing through the face, and lightly scoring the core. Now stand the panel upright, grab the edge, and steadily push it back until the piece snaps along the score mark. Then cut through the backing paper on the back side.

For small and irregular cuts, use a drywall or keyhole saw. Make larger openings with a circle cutter. You can smooth rough edges with a drywall rasp or surface-forming tool.

Hanging

Generally, pros prefer to hang drywall sheets horizontally, starting at the top and working down the wall. The long tapered edges make shallow troughs that let you create virtually invisible seams. Try to locate untapered, or butt, edges in corners or at floor or ceiling level.

Drywall the ceiling first, then the walls. Space nails or screws no more than 6 inches apart along each ceiling joist, and 8 inches apart along wall studs. You can drive nails with a drywall hammer or an ordinary hammer. For screws, buy or rent an electric drywall screw gun. These have a special nosing around the bit that allows the screws to be driven to a certain depth and no farther. Whichever fastening method you choose, screws or nails, the goal is the same. You want to set the fasteners below the surface, but not so far the paper facing tears.

Make sure each fastener hits a stud. Any fastener that misses the framing needs to be pulled out and the hole filled with joint compound. If you leave fasteners that miss, they'll pop back out someday.

Drive drywall fasteners into the framing or they will pop back out sometime down the road. Mark the locations of studs and joists before lifting a panel into place.

Raise lower panels up against the panels above with a foot lift or a prybar. Base molding will cover the gap at floor level.

Nails vs. screws

Which work better? Screws have greater holding power and are less likely to pop out later. A hammer, on the other hand, extends your reach – an important consideration when you're driving fasteners up at the ceiling line.

Of course there's no law that says you can't use both. Some pros like to nail panel edges and screw along intermediate studs.

It makes those first few screws or nails a lot easier to drive if you start them before lifting the panel into place.

Dimple the fasteners so they can be covered over with joint compound. In other words, drive them below the drywall surface, but not so far that they break the paper facing. A drywall hammer has a rounded face that makes this easier.

Attach drywall to studs with drywall nails, or drive drywall screws with an electric drywall screw gun. Use a drywall rasp to smooth rough edges.

Paper tape or mesh?

Many do-it-yourselfers prefer mesh tape because its adhesive backing makes it easy to apply. However, paper tape is the better choice for a drywall installation for several reasons.

- With paper tape you can use any joint compound, including ready-mixed. Mesh tape should only be used with setting-type compounds, which have to be mixed on site.
- Paper tape makes a stronger joint; with the proper application of three coats of mud, paper tape joints become as strong as the wallboard. Joints made with mesh tape are prone to cracking.
- Paper tape is easier to crease around corners.
- Paper tape is cheaper.

Taping and mudding joints

Start with the untapered butt joints. Load a 5- or 6-inch broad knife with joint compound (commonly called mud) and apply a thin, even coat along the length of the joint. Hold the knife at a 45-degree angle and draw it down the seam in one continuous motion.

After you lay on this first coat of mud, cut a strip of paper tape the length of the joint and lightly press the tape into the wet joint compound with your fingers. Now, load some more mud on the knife, then draw it firmly along the joint to embed the tape. After each pass, scrape off any mud that remains on the knife. Debris on the knife will leave lumps in your work.

Follow the same procedure with tapered joints. Wherever taper joints meet butt joints, run the tape on the taper joint over the tape on the butt joint.

After taping the joints, fill each nail or screw dimple with compound, too. Use a continuous pass of the knife to level a whole row of dimples at a time.

1 *Lay on the first coat* of joint compound with a broad knife. Use short strokes to fill the joint. Don't worry about smoothing the joint until after the tape is embedded.

2 *Cut a strip of tape* to length and press it into the mud.

Taping and mudding corners

At inside corners, apply a thin layer of compound on both sides. Cut a strip of tape, crease it lengthwise, and lightly press it into the corner with your fingers. Load up the knife with more mud and draw it down each side to embed the tape.

Outside corners must first be reinforced with corner bead – lightweight perforated metal that you cut with tin snips and tack in place with drywall nails. Apply the mud with horizontal passes from the wall toward the bead, then level the mud with a continuous

3 *Load up your knife* with more mud and draw it along the joint to embed the tape and force out any air bubbles. For a smooth joint, hold the knife at an angle and pull it along the joint in one continuous motion.

4 *Apply the second and third coats*, feathering the joint out a little farther with each coat. Allow each coat to dry completely before applying the next one. (Note the row of fastener dimples. Each was filled individually, then the whole row was leveled with one pass of the blade.)

stroke. Hold the knife at a 45-degree angle with one edge overhanging the metal bead.

Finish coats

Let the first coat dry overnight. Then lightly scrape off bumps, ridges, and other imperfections with the broad knife. While you've got the broad knife out, put a second coat of mud over the fasteners.

Now switch to an 8- or 10-inch taping knife and apply a second coat of mud to tapered joints. Make two overlapping passes to feather out the mud so it extends beyond the first coat for a total width of 7 or 8 inches. With butt joints, feather the compound even farther to a total width of 14 inches. Apply the third coat after the second one is dry, using a 10- or 12-inch knife and feathering the joints out even more.

At inside corners, use a broad knife to apply a second coat to just one side of the corner. Let the compound dry overnight. Coat the other side of the corner when you apply the third coat to the seams. Inside corners end up with just two coats of mud.

5 *A pole sander* extends your reach and saves your back. Use fine-grit sandpaper or sanding screen, and sand lightly to avoid scuffing the paper facing. Be sure to wear safety glasses and a dust mask.

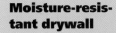

Installing Backer Board

Hanging and mudding backer board calls for techniques similar to those used for installing drywall, but requires different materials. Backer board seams are covered with a fiberglass mesh tape, not paper tape, and seams are filled with thinset mortar, not joint compound.

Because they measure 3x4, 3x5, and 3x6 feet, backer board panels fit most tub/shower walls with a minimum of cutting and mudding. And because they're the same ½ inch thickness as standard drywall, you can neatly butt the two materials together.

Cutting

To trim panels to size, lay them flat – you'll need plenty of leverage to cut through the fiberglass mesh facing and score the cement core underneath. Set a T-square along the cutting line then score the line with a carbide-tipped scoring knife. You'll need to make several passes.

Now snap the panel at the line. After the core breaks, slice through the mesh backing with a utility knife.

Hanging

Nail up panels with 1½-inch galvanized roofing nails spaced 8 inches apart. Or use 1¼- or 1⅝-inch galvanized backer board screws spaced 8 inches apart. Nail and screw heads should be flush with – not below – the surface.

Taping and mudding

Unlike drywall joints, the seams between backer board panels don't have to be invisible. After all, you'll be covering them up with tile later on. The seams must be level, though, or you'll have trouble keeping the tiles on the same plane.

Prefill the joints with thinset mortar, press fiberglass mesh tape into them, embed the tape, and level the joints.

1 *To cut backer board*, first score it using a carbide-tipped scoring knife. Snap the panel to break the core along the score mark, then cut the backing with a utility knife.

2 *Shave off any rough edges* with a utility knife or a carbide-tipped scoring knife. You should also shave down the edge of any panel that doesn't quite fit, forcing it in will crumble the edge.

Cutting holes in backer board

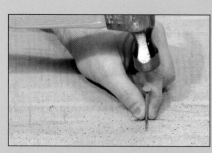

1 *To make holes* in backer board, drive a nail where the hole will be centered. Pull the nail, then mark the cutout on both sides with a scribing compass, using the nail hole as a reference.

2 *Use a carbide-tipped* scoring knife to score along the outline on both sides.

3 *Smack out the hole* with a hammer and smooth the cutout with the scoring knife.

3 *Install panels* smooth side out if you plan to put up tiles with adhesive, rough side out for bonding with thinset mortar. Leave a ¼-inch gap at the top of the tub to allow for expansion and contraction.

4 *Drive* fasteners into studs at 8-inch intervals. Use either galvanized roofing nails or backer board screws.

5 *Using a broad knife*, spread a generous coat of thinset along the seam.

6 *Lightly press* a length of fiberglass mesh tape into the seam.

7 *Embed the tape* and smooth the joint with the broad knife. Thinset will ooze up through the mesh tape, so you probably won't have to load more thinset on your knife to embed the tape.

Smooth side or rough side out?

If you plan to set tiles with mastic, install the backer board panels smooth side out; if you plan to set the tiles with thinset, hang the panels rough side out. The rule of thumb is to use mastic for setting tile on vertical surfaces and thinset for tiles set on horizontal planes. To be safe, check the tile manufacturer's recommendation on adhesives before installing the backer board.

Installing a Fiberglass Tub Surround

To make cutouts for the showerhead, faucet, and spout you first need to make a template. Trim cardboard to the size of the panel, carefully position it, then press it against the pipes and faucets. They'll make indentations in the cardboard that show where to make the cutouts.

Next, check to be sure your template fits, then tape it to the face of the panel and trace the cutting lines onto the panel.

Use a caulk gun to apply adhesive to the walls. After the adhesive dries to the consistency recommended by the manufacturer, press the panels into place. Leave a ¼-inch gap between the bottom of each panel and the top of the tub.

Install the corner moldings, then improvise a 2x4 brace to hold the panels in place until the adhesive cures.

Finally, seal around the fittings, along the top of the tub, and along the moldings with silicone caulk.

1 *Make a template* for the wall at the head of the tub. Test-fit the template before you transfer cutouts for the fittings from the template to the panel.

2 *Cut holes* with the panel facing up. For a large hole, first bore a starter hole with a drill, then cut the opening with a jig saw. Make smaller holes with a hole saw or a spade bit.

3 *Apply adhesive* according to the manufacturer's directions. Provide plenty of ventilation – the vapors from most mastics are toxic.

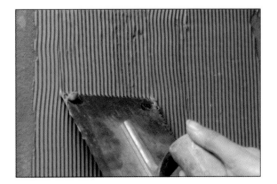

4 *Comb out the adhesive* with a notched trowel, unless the manufacturer recommends otherwise. The ridges provide a tight grip when you press the panels into place.

5 *Brace the surround* with scrap lumber until the adhesive has cured thoroughly, usually 24 hours or so. Bridge contours in the panels by using a combination of long and short pieces of lumber.

Ceramic tile is pretty easy to work with. *You'll need to buy or rent some specialized tools, but none are difficult to operate.*

Regardless of whether you're tiling walls, a floor, or a countertop, budget several days for the project. First you need to provide a sturdy base for the installation. Next you lay out the job and establish guidelines to ensure that everything will come out even. Then you bond the tiles to the base, pack the joints with grout, and finally, caulk joints and seal the grout.

Tiling a Floor

A ceramic tile floor is only as good as the surface that's underneath it. You need an underlayment that's even, solid, and absolutely rigid. Install tiles over anything else and you can expect problems later on.

Two underlayments that meet these guidelines are backer board and mortar beds (also called mud beds). Because a mud bed is best installed by a masonry or tile contractor, most do-it-yourselfers opt for a backer board underlayment. Use ½-inch-thick backer board unless the backer board combined with the thinset and tile will raise the floor height too much. In that case, use 5/16-inch-thick backer board.

Installing backer board

Cutting backer board requires two knives: a carbide-tipped scoring knife and a utility knife. Score one side of the backer board with the scoring knife, snap the core, then use the utility knife to cut through the mesh backing.

To fasten backer board to the floor, first lay down a coat of thinset adhesive – you'll use the same stuff later to set the tile – and comb it out with a ¼-inch notched trowel. Then drive backer board screws or 1½-inch galvanized roofing nails spaced 8 inches apart along all edges and in the field.

Finally, fill the seams with more thinset and some fiberglass mesh tape. Let the thinset cure overnight.

1 *Score one side* of the backer board with a carbide-tipped scoring knife. You can also cut backer board with a circular saw and carbide-tipped blade. (To cut holes in backer board see page 62.)

2 *Cut the mesh facing* with a utility knife after snapping the cement core along the score mark.

3 *Use thinset adhesive* to bond backer board to the subfloor. Spread the thinset with the smooth edge of a square-notched floor trowel, then comb it out with the notched edge.

4 *Fasten the backer board* to the subfloor with backer board screws or galvanized roofing nails. Space the fasteners 8 inches apart along the edges and in the field.

5 *Trowel thinset* into each seam. Then apply fiberglass mesh tape, using a broad knife to embed the tape and level the seam.

Planning the layout

Start your layout grid by snapping a chalk line parallel to and one tile width away from the tub (or doorway). The line should extend to opposite walls. To help position the chalk line, place a tile at each end of the tub (or doorway), leaving a grout space between the tub (or doorway) and the tiles.

Place tiles along the length of this line, leaving grout space between tiles. Now, how do they look? Shift the tiles a few inches one way or the other to center them between walls – especially if you'll end up with less than half a tile at one wall or the other.

When you're satisfied with the tile layout along the first line, use a square to snap a second chalkline perpendicular to the first. Position the second line between two of the tiles along the first line. Set out more tiles along the second line, then check for balanced cuts and tile alignment. Keep ad-

justing the tiles along both lines until you are pleased with how the entire layout looks.

Then use the square and chalkline to mark a grid across the entire floor. The grid helps you keep tiles straight and evenly spaced. Size the sections of the grid to accommodate whole tiles and the spaces between them. Each section should be no bigger than 2- to 3-feet square.

Layout lines ensure that tiles will be square with the room's most prominent feature; in a bathroom this is usually along the base of the tub or at the doorway. For visual reasons, you'll want to lay as few cut tiles here as possible.

Mud beds

For an absolutely smooth, level, rock-solid ceramic tile floor, some contractors pour a ¾- to 1-inch-thick mortar mud bed. Even if you've worked with concrete outdoors, don't try to float a mortar bed unless you're really sure of your abilities –

it's a tricky process best left to professionals. A mortar bed begins with a layer of roofing felt topped with wire mesh to reinforce the mortar.

The mud is mixed to just the right dry, crumbling consistency, which takes a practiced eye.

After the mud is poured, it has to be firmly packed down.

Next the bed is leveled, a process called screeding.

Finally, the mortar is troweled smooth and left to cure overnight.

Setting field tile

Thinset is the adhesive to use for setting floor tile. It comes as a powder that you mix with either water or a liquid latex additive. Thinset dries quickly, so work in just one grid section at a time. Start in the far corner and work your way toward the door so you won't have to walk on freshly set tiles.

Spread some thinset with the straight edge of a square-notched flooring trowel. Then hold the trowel at a 45-degree angle and drag the notched edge across it to create ridges in the thinset.

Next, align a tile with the intersection of two chalklines and set it in place, twisting slightly to provide good contact between the tile and adhesive. It's a good idea to pull up this first tile and check that its underside is uniformly covered with adhesive. If there's little adhesive on the tile back, you need to spread more thinset and/or raise the angle of the trowel to get higher ridges. If there's too much adhesive you should apply less and/or lower the angle of the trowel to make lower ridges.

Build outward from the first tile, eyeballing the grout spaces. After you've laid all the full tiles that will fit in a section, tamp them into the mortar with a rubber mallet, and do one last check on tile spacing and alignment. Then remove any excess thinset that oozed up between the tiles.

Cutting and setting edge tiles

Some do-it-yourselfers set all the field tiles first, then go back to cut and fit partial tiles around the edges. Others prefer to cut and fit as they go.

2 *Set the first tile* in place, give it a quick twist to ensure good contact, and adjust it so it's even with the chalk lines. Accuracy is important here because this tile serves as a keystone for the others.

1 *Spread thinset* with the straight side of a trowel, then make ridges with the notched edge. The adhesive should be just wet enough to hold ridges and adhere to the tile.

5 *Take careful measurements* for each cut tile you'll need. Few rooms are perfectly square so the size of the cut tiles will change as you work your way along the wall.

Whichever method you choose, measure carefully for each individual tile, allowing for grout spaces between the tiles and along the walls. Don't assume that all the edge tiles will be the same width; unless the room is perfectly square – and few are – edge tiles will change size as you move along the wall.

Make straight cuts for edge tiles with either a manual tile cutter or an electric wet saw (also called a tub saw). Both are available at rental centers. The manual cutter works well and will be reasonably cheap to rent. The tub saw might be worth the additional rental fee if you have to make tons of cuts or particularly intricate cuts. To keep the cost down, set all the full tiles, then rent the tub saw and start working on the cut tiles. Save time by working as a team; one person measures and sets cut tiles while the other operates the saw.

Do you really need tile spacers?

Most wall tiles have lugs on their edges that maintain space between them for grout; most floor tiles do not. You can buy or improvise spacers to stick between floor tiles, but if you lay out a grid, there's no need to waste time placing – and later removing – tile spacers. Instead, just follow your grid lines and eyeball the spacing.

If you don't trust what you're seeing, double-check the tile alignment with a story pole. You can make your own from a straight board by making marks the width of grout lines, spaced exactly a tile width apart.

3 **Now build out** from either side of the first tile. Align the tile edges, leaving spaces between them for grout.

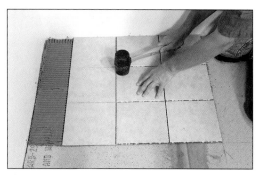

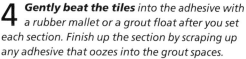

4 **Gently beat the tiles** into the adhesive with a rubber mallet or a grout float after you set each section. Finish up the section by scraping up any adhesive that oozes into the grout spaces.

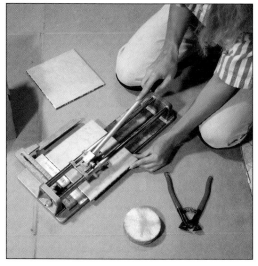

6 **To cut a tile** on a manual tile cutter, position the tile on the table, pull the scoring wheel across it, then push down on the lever to snap the tile in two. Polish the cut edge with a rub stone.

7 **Carefully align** the cut tile and drop it in place with the cut edge toward the wall. Be sure to leave grout space between tiles as well as a ¼-inch space between the tile and wall.

Making irregular cuts

Here you have several choices, depending on how neat you want the cut. For cuts that won't show, such as around a toilet flange, use tile nippers. These take tiny bites out of a tile, which leaves a rough edge.

A rod saw makes more precise cuts. It consists of a special carbide blade that fits into a hacksaw frame. Use a rod saw to make curved cuts along a tile's edge, or to cut holes in tile. To cut a hole, drill a small starter hole with a carbide-tipped bit, remove the rod saw blade from the frame, thread the blade through the hole, reassemble the saw, and cut out the hole.

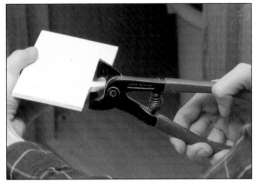

Use tile nippers to make cuts that will be hidden under toilets, faucet escutcheons, and other places where looks don't matter. To avoid breaking tiles, always take small bites with nippers.

A rod saw consists of a round, carbide-coated blade that mounts in a hacksaw frame. Use it to make curved cuts along the edge of a tile.

Cut circles with a rod saw, too. First, drill a hole in the tile with a carbide bit. Release the blade, thread it through the hole, and re-tension the blade.

Saw around the outline, starting from the hole you drilled. For even tighter cuts, you also can buy rod saw blades that fit coping saw frames.

Tub saws make quick work of straight cuts. The blade has a diamond cutting edge and a water spray to keep the blade's temperature down. These saws are messy and noisy, so work outside or in the garage. Wear hearing protection and safety glasses.

1 **Spread grout** over the tiles with a rubber grout float. Hold the float at about a 30-degree angle and make diagonal strokes to force grout into the spaces between tiles. Remove excess grout holding the float almost perpendicular to the tile.

Grouting

Wall and floor tiles require different grout formulations. Why? Because wall tiles are usually spaced ⅛ inch or less and should be grouted with a plain, unsanded grout. Wider joints, such as those typically seen with floor tiles, are weaker and require a grout that has sand mixed in for added strength.

Both plain and sanded grout come as a powder that you mix on site. Use liquid latex additive to mix grouts for surfaces that are often wet, such as floors, shower walls, and countertops. Besides increasing water resistance, latex additives also make grout joints more flexible, which minimizes cracking.

Check the directions before using a latex grout additive. Many manufacturers now add dry latex polymers to their grout mixes. Grouts with dry polymers should be mixed only with water, not liquid latex additives.

2 **Wipe grout off** the tiles with a damp – not wet – grout sponge. Use a grout sponge with rounded edges; it's less likely to drag grout of the joints. Use light, circular strokes and rinse the sponge frequently.

3 **Lightly smooth** the grout joints with the edge of the sponge. Use a barely damp, clean sponge. Then make a final cleaning pass over the tiles. Using slow, steady strokes, make only one pass with each side of the sponge, then rinse and continue.

4 **A thin grout haze** will form on the tiles after about 15 minutes. Use a clean, soft cloth to polish it off. Don't let the haze sit too long or it will be hard to remove. Try a plastic scouring pad on tough spots of dried grout.

Tiling Walls

Field tiles make up the bulk of a wall installation, but you'll also need an assortment of trim tiles to finish off edges and create accents. Trim tiles are sold by the piece or by the running foot.

Use bullnose tiles to finish the perimeter. While you can also use bullnose tiles to round over an outside corner, some tile manufacturers make trim tiles specially designed for use at corners.

Insert ¹⁄₁₆-inch spacers between trim tiles to make room for grout. You probably won't have to do this for the field tiles because most field tiles are self-spacing.

Use a level to mark horizontal and vertical working lines for each wall. In a shower, tile to a height that's at least 6 inches above the showerhead.

Spread mastic in a 3- by 3-foot area with the straight edge of a V-notched trowel, then comb it into ridges with the notched edge. Don't cover up your working lines.

Position field tiles and gently press them into place. Don't use a twisting motion, as you would with floor tiles. If adhesive oozes out, clean it up right away.

Cut and set tiles around plumbing stubouts as you go; straight cuts, such as those in the corner, can wait until the end if you prefer. (See pages 69–70 to learn about cutting tile.)

Layout

Grout lines that aren't perfectly plumb and level – and horizontal grout lines that don't line up in the corner – will bug you every time you look at them, so take the time to draw level and plumb working lines.

Start with the long wall of the tub surround. Lay a level on the tub's top edge and find its lowest point. Set a tile there on top of a ¼-inch spacer and mark the wall at the top of the tile. From this mark extend a level line across the wall. If the tub is not level, most tiles below this line will have to be cut to fit.

Now find the center of the wall and prop tiles from there to each wall. If you'll end up with less than half a tile at the ends, shift the row a half-tile width. In other words, if you started out with a joint centered on the line, shift the layout so that a tile is centered on the line.

Once you're happy with the horizontal layout, use a level to draw a vertical layout line that's near the center of the wall and aligned with the edge of one of the tiles. Then draw a level line to mark the top of the tile installation.

Finally, mark the location of any accessories, such as soap dishes, that will be adhered to the backer board.

Setting the tile

Spread mastic onto the wall, then comb it out with a V-notched trowel. Work in sections about three feet square, but don't apply any adhesive where accessories will go.

Starting at the bottom of the wall, carefully align each tile and press it into the adhesive. Start each row along the center line and work out to the edges. Immediately clean off any adhesive that oozes up into grout spaces.

Back-buttering tiles

With back-buttering, adhesive is applied directly to the tile back and combed out with the short side of the notched trowel. Back-butter whenever you're setting individual tiles after the rest of the installation is completed (accessories, trim tiles, and replacement tiles, for example). Some tiles, including very small pieces of tile or rough-backed tiles, require back-buttering in addition to the adhesive applied to the substrate to ensure that they will bond.

Apply silicone adhesive to the back of soap dishes and other accessories. Set accessories after the grout cures.

Press the soap dish in place, then secure it with tape. After the adhesive dries – usually 24 hours – remove the tape. (Note that while most soap dishes are adhered to the tile substrate, the type shown here can be glued right to the tile.)

Back-butter sanitary base tiles and stick them to the wall. Shim each tile ⅛ inch above the floor; this gap will be caulked after the tiles are grouted. Sanitary base tiles add a nice touch, even when the flooring is vinyl. Choose tiles with bullnose edges if you won't be tiling the walls and floor, too.

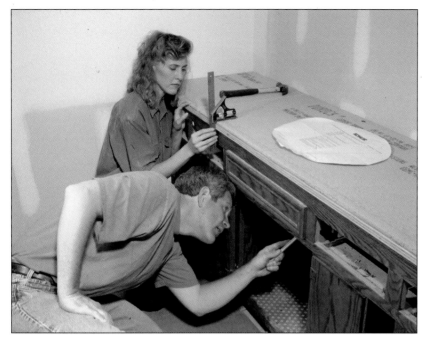

1 *Trace the sink opening* in the plywood base onto the bottom of the backer board, then flip the backer board over.

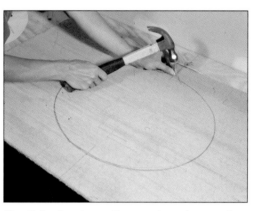

2 *Drive locator nails* spaced evenly around the perimeter of the cutout. Pull them out, then score along the outline with a carbide-tipped scoring knife.

3 *Turn the board over* again and use the nail holes to align the template. Trace around it, score along the line, then tap around the edge with a hammer until the cutout drops out.

Tiling a Countertop

A sturdy countertop begins with a solid substrate. After you've installed the cabinets (see pages 82–83), cut a sheet of ¾-inch exterior grade plywood to fit over the cabinets, then attach it by screwing up through the corner blocks inside the cabinets. The second layer of the substrate is ½-inch-thick cement backer board. Cut the backer board to size and set it aside for now.

Making a sink cutout

Use the template that came with the sink to mark the sink's location on the plywood. Cut the sink opening with a jig saw.

To cut the backer board, you'll have to score the opening on both sides with a carbide-tipped scoring knife, then tap the cutout loose with a hammer. To make sure the score marks on both sides line up, trace the opening onto one side, drive nails through the backer board at several points along the line, then flip the board over and use the nail holes as markers to position the template and mark the second side.

Laminate the backer board to the plywood with thinset, then drive galvanized roofing nails or backer board screws every 8 inches in the field and along the edges. Tape and mud any seams as shown on page 66.

Layout

Before you set any tile, plan the layout by doing a dry run. First set out all the edge tiles. Shift the row of tile back and forth until

4 *Dry lay tiles* across the edges and front to back. This shows where you'll need to make cuts. If you end up with less than half a tile at the edge, shift the layout over by half a tile width.

there are equal-sized pieces at both ends, and no small slivers of tile. Now lay out a row of tiles from the edge tile back to the wall. Generally, you want a full tile at the front edge of the counter, with the cut tiles falling along the back where they'll be less visible.

Next, fill in some more field tiles (remember to leave spaces for grout between them) so you can check how the cut tiles will fall around the sink. Try to avoid small slivers of tile around the sink. When the layout looks good to you, use a framing square and chalk line to mark reference lines on the backer board.

Setting the tile

Spread thinset over the backer board and comb ridges into it with a square-notched trowel. Set the edge tiles first.

Next set all the full field tiles. Cut and set the tiles around the sink opening as you come to them. You can either set the cut tiles along the back edge as you go or wait until the end, then cut and set them all at once. If you save the cut tiles for last, don't spread any thinset where they will go; it will film over before you get around to cutting and setting those tiles. Instead, backbutter the cut tiles as you set them. (To learn about cutting tiles, see pages 69–70.) After the adhesive sets up, grout the countertop as shown on page 71.

5 **Set the edge tiles** first. Align them with the reference line and be sure to leave space for grout between tiles.

6 **Silicone adhesive holds** edge tiles in place until the thinset cures. Backbutter the edge tile using silicone behind the face and thinset under the top, then press the tile onto the substrate.

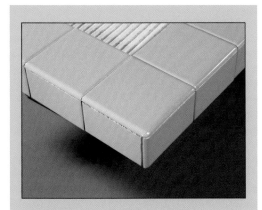

Another way to trim edges

Bullnose tiles also make an attractive countertop edge treatment. First, cut partial tiles to the edge's thickness and adhere them to the front face with silicone adhesive. Then set bullnose tiles on top of the counter so they overlap the cut edge tiles. Use double bullnose tiles for corners.

7 **Lay the full field tiles**, as well as the cut tiles around the sink opening. Finish up by cutting and setting partial tiles at the back of the counter. Make curved cuts with nippers or a rod saw; use a tile snapper for the straight cuts (see pages 69–70).

Fighting gravity

To help hold edge tiles in place until the thinset cures, set the tiles with a combination of silicone adhesive and thinset. Silicon adhesive sets up faster than thinset, so it holds the tile in place until the thinset cures. Apply silicone adhesive to bond the vertical face of the V-cap tile, and thinset to bond the horizontal surface.

Finishing Up

At this point your tile job may look done – but it's not. You have to caulk any open joints and seal the grout before you can say you are finished.

Caulk

Caulk provides a flexible seal between materials that expand and contract at different rates. Also use it to fill joints where one surface is subjected to forces or movement that the other is not. For example, when you stand in a tub or fill it with water, the tub will drop a tiny fraction of an inch; step out or pull the plug and it will rise again. A bead of caulk rides out these ups and downs.

Caulk around all tub edges, where tile walls meet in inside corners, between the tub and a tile floor, between floor and wall tiles, where counters meet backsplashes, and between tile and cabinets. Try pushing the caulk gun instead of pulling it; that forces more caulk into the joint you are filling.

Choose a silicone caulk that's the same color as the grout you used, but wait until the grout has cured to apply it.

Sealing grout

Silicone grout sealer makes grout joints easier to clean. Let the joints cure for several weeks, then seal them according to instructions on the applicator. You will need to reapply grout sealer about once a year or so.

Maintain steady pressure and keep the caulk gun moving at a rate that fills the crack without overflowing. Either fill the tub or stand in it when caulking between a tub and its surround.

Wet your fingertip and run it along the caulk. The goal is to end up with a neat, slightly concave bead.

Grout is porous, so it accumulates dirt and mildew over time. To make grout easier to clean, treat it with silicone sealer.

Keeping caulk from creeping

One frustrating thing about caulking ceramic tile is that the caulk sneaks up into grout joints when you smooth out the bead, leaving a wavy looking line. To keep this from happening, apply strips of masking tape on both sides of the joint you want to caulk and smooth them down tightly. Caulk, level the compound with your finger, pull off the tape, and there you go – a nice, straight bead of caulk across the tiles and grout joints.

VINYL FLOORING

The wide variety of vinyl flooring available gives you more choice than ever in pattern, quality, and price, but it also creates more installation options. Depending on the manufacturer and the type of flooring, different installation techniques and materials may be required for what appear to be very similar products. Make sure to read the manufacturer's installation instructions. If the process recommended by the manufacturer differs from what you read here, go with the manufacturer's guidelines. Using an installation method or adhesive other than that recommended by the flooring manufacturer could void the warranty.

Underlayment

If you lay vinyl flooring on an uneven or unsound base, or over heavily cushioned or embossed flooring, any imperfections will eventually telegraph through to the new flooring. To be safe, install a new underlayment of ¼-inch lauan plywood.

After leveling any low spots, lay out the sheets of lauan so the seams are staggered and centered over joists. Fasten the lauan with narrow-crown staples, screws, or ring-shank nails. Sink the fastener heads below the surface (take care not to drive screws right through the lauan). Fill all seams and screw and nail heads (but not staple heads) with leveling compound.

Drive narrow-crown staples *every 2 to 4 inches along panel edges and in the field. Tight spacing helps keep the lauan from buckling when exposed to moisture, including the moisture in the flooring adhesive.*

Fill low spots *with leveling compound before installing the new underlayment. Lauan doesn't provide structural strength, just a smooth surface for the new flooring. It will sag or flex into any low spots, which will weaken the seams.*

Fill the seams *between panels with floor-leveling compound. After the compound dries, smooth it with an orbital sander.*

Installing vinyl tile

Lay tiles one quadrant *at a time, starting in the corner and working back and forth between the lines. Pay attention to pattern matching as you lay each tile; some tiles have arrows on the paper backing to help you out. Finish up by rolling the floor with a rented 100-pound floor roller to force out the air bubbles and set the adhesive.*

When you install vinyl tile, planning and laying out your installation is the lion's share of the job. Start by snapping chalk lines that divide the floor into equal-sized quadrants. Check your chalk lines to make sure they're perfectly square. Then test-lay tiles along the lines. If the tiles at the edges come out less than half a tile wide, or are different sizes, keep moving the lines of tile back and forth and up and down until you like what you see, then snap new chalk lines.

Before setting any tile, check that all boxes have the same lot number.

To cut border tiles, *lay a loose tile directly over the last full tile. Carefully set a third tile on top, butted against the wall. Use the top tile to mark the cut line on the middle tile.*

Make a template from heavy-duty paper and duct tape. A steel straightedge and utility knife will help you make precise cuts at doorways and corners.

Tape the template to the vinyl every few feet along the edges and at all cutouts to keep the template from slipping while you cut the vinyl.

Use a utility knife with a sharp, new blade, and proceed slowly and deliberately as you make your cuts. Hold the knife perfectly vertical so your cuts don't slant one way or the other.

Installing sheet vinyl

The day before the installation, bring the flooring and adhesive inside so they can acclimate. Unroll sheet goods so the flooring will lay flat when you cut it. Be careful not to crease or kink the flooring when you unroll it.

Make a template

In case the corners of the room aren't exactly square, it's a good idea to make your template a bit longer and wider than the room, then trim it to size. Also, cut small holes every few feet. You'll use these later, when you tape the template to the vinyl.

Cutting the vinyl

If your template is accurate, the biggest problem you'll have cutting the flooring will be finding the space to roll it out flat. The best place to do this is in an adjacent room, garage, or basement. Make sure the surface is clean – stray stones or gravel can pit or dent sheet vinyl.

After taping together any seams, position the template over the vinyl. If the template doesn't square to the vinyl's pattern, adjust the position of the template so the most visible edge in the room (probably the doorway and/or the front edge of the tub) runs square to the pattern. Tape down the template, then cut out the vinyl.

How to seam sheet vinyl

Overlap the two pieces of vinyl so that the pattern matches in both directions. Hide the seam along the edge of a "grout line" or another strong linear design element. Check that the pattern aligns along the entire seam, then tape the seam securely. After cutting and gluing the seam, apply the seam sealer recommended by the manufacturer.

What is template paper?

You can use any heavy paper to make a template. Many flooring manufacturers sell template kits that come with paper. Otherwise, check home centers or art supply stores for resin paper, kraft paper, butcher paper, or any other heavy paper that won't stretch or leave marks on the vinyl.

Spreading adhesive is more manageable if you fold the vinyl back on itself and apply adhesive to one half of the floor at a time. After the flooring is glued down, go over it with a 100-pound floor roller to force out air bubbles and ensure a good bond. A heavy rolling pin works well in tight spots.

Comb the adhesive into ridges with a notched trowel. Unless the manufacturer specifies otherwise, use a trowel with a ¹/₁₆ inch V-notch. Be sure to ventilate the room when working with adhesive.

Perimeter bond vinyl

Perimeter bond vinyl goes down fast because you apply adhesive only under seams and around the edges. You can even staple the edges instead of gluing them if the staples will be hidden under base molding. Use ½-inch-crown staples with at least a ⅜-inch leg, spaced 3 inches apart. If there's a seam, cut and glue the seam before fastening the perimeter. Roll the seam and glued edges with a J-roller.

Fully adhered vinyl

Gluing down fully adhered vinyl is easier if you work on just half the room at a time. However, don't spread any adhesive within a foot of any seam line; the seam is cut and glued after the rest of the flooring.

Finishing

If the walls already have a wood baseboard, conceal the flooring edges by adding base-shoe molding. Fasten the molding with 6-penny finishing nails driven into the wall studs, not the floor.

Another option is to install a cove molding of vinyl strip or ceramic tile. Follow the manufacturer's directions for installing vinyl cove molding; see page 73 for ceramic tile cove base installation.

A beveled wood threshold eases the transition between different floor heights in adjacent rooms. To install a wood threshold, trim the door stops so the threshold will fit beneath them. Then drill pilot holes and fasten the threshold with 8-penny finishing nails.

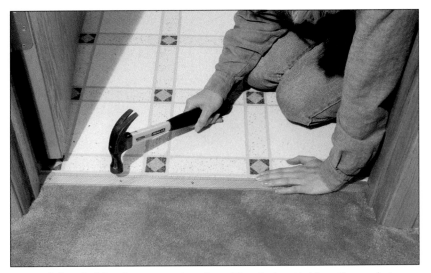

A metal threshold strip protects the edge of the vinyl and bridges the gap between different flooring materials. Cut it to length with a hacksaw, and nail it in place with the supplied nails.

Two important words about doing the finish work – be gentle. *Chip a sink, overtighten a fitting, crack a toilet or mirror, and it's back to the home center you go. To ensure that doesn't happen to you, follow a few common-sense precautions.*

Keep the floor clear of anything you could stumble over. Good advice for any phase of a remodeling project, but especially important when you're carrying costly components.

Do as much as you can elsewhere. Unpack and preassemble items in another room or outside, where you have more room to maneuver.

Don't rush. If you're running out of time or patience, take a break. With finish work, haste does make waste.

Installing Cabinets

Begin the installation with a dry run to make sure all the cabinets fit. After the dry run, move the other cabinets out of the way and start the installation with the sink cabinet.

Filler strips

If the cabinet run falls a couple inches short of the wall, fill the gap with a matching filler strip. Scribe and rip the filler strip to the right width, clamp it to the cabinet, then drive screws through the stile into the strip. (To learn about scribing, see page 87.)

Wall cabinets

Wait to install a cabinet over the toilet until just about everything else is done. Then draw a level line where the bottom edge of the cabinet will be. (The rule of thumb is to center the cabinet over the toilet, high enough to allow easy access to the tank.) Screw a 1x2 cleat to the wall to support the base of the cabinet during installation. Drive screws through the hanging rail into the studs, then remove the cleat and patch the holes.

Finishing

Wait until the bathroom is almost finished to install the cabinet doors, shelves, and drawers. It'll be easier to install the countertop, sink, and faucet if they're out of the way, and they're less likely to be damaged in the process.

1 ***Few floors are level****, so find and mark the highest point in the floor. All the cabinets will be shimmed up to this height to make a level run of cabinets.*

2 ***Measure up*** *from the high point to determine where cabinet tops will line up. Standard vanity cabinets are 30 inches high.*

Cabinets and ceramic tile floors

If you're installing resilient flooring, lay the floor first, then set cabinets on top of it. But if your plans call for ceramic tile, set the cabinets first using shims to raise the cabinets to the height of the finish flooring. Then put down backer board underlayment and tile up to the cabinet edges.

3 ***Use a level*** *to mark the cabinets' top line. Work to this line, shimming the cabinets underneath as necessary.*

4 **Set the cabinet** in place after cutting any openings needed for the plumbing. Always remove the doors, shelves, and drawers and put them somewhere out of the way. This keeps them from being damaged and makes it easier to install the cabinets.

8 **Shim the second cabinet** up to the line, level it, then clamp the cabinets together. (Note the filler strip between cabinets. Because of the molding on the cabinet edges, this particular model of cabinet requires a spacer between cabinets.)

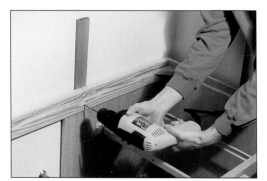

9 **Screw the cabinets together** through the face-frame stiles. A combination bit drills the pilot hole and the counterbore in one operation. Try to position the screws so they'll be hidden behind the door hinges whenever possible.

10 **Install** a large cabinet like this linen cabinet the same as any other; level and plumb it with shims, then screw through the hanging rails at the top, middle, and bottom. Anchor it to at least two wall studs.

5 **Set a level** on top of the cabinet and check that the cabinet is level front to back along each side, and side to side across the front and rear.

6 **Use shims to level** the cabinet and bring it up to the 30-inch line on the wall. Later, trim off the shims with a chisel.

7 **Drill pilot holes**, then drive 2½-inch screws through the hanging rail into each stud. If there's a gap between the cabinet and the wall, put a shim in it before driving the screws, otherwise the cabinet will be pulled out of square.

Safe work space

If you decide to do your own laminate work, don't plan to do it in the bathroom. You'll need more space, and fumes from the contact cement used to glue down the laminate are toxic and flammable. Work only in an open, well-ventilated area away from an open flame or pilot light, preferably in a garage or even outdoors.

Fabricating a Laminate Countertop

Laminate countertop construction starts with the base: ¾-inch particleboard. Cut the top to size, allowing a 1-inch overhang at the front and exposed sides. Next, glue and screw 4-inch-wide build-up strips of particleboard to the underside. These strips, which rest on the cabinet edges, add rigidity and provide a 1½-inch-thick edge to the finished counter. To compensate for the strips, narrow strips of particleboard are glued and nailed to the cabinet tops to support the rest of the countertop.

Cut ¾-inch particleboard to the size of the cabinet, plus a 1-inch overhang on all sides that won't be against a wall. Build up the edges with build-up strips glued and screwed to the underside.

Fill the gap between the cabinet and the substrate with ¾-inch wood strips fastened to the top of the cabinet sides. Put a strip along the back edge of the cabinet, too.

Lay a bead of white glue on the cabinet edges and press the strips into the glue. Drive 4-penny finishing nails through the strips into the cabinet edges.

Fabricating a solid-surface countertop

Don't try this at home. Constructing custom solid-surface counters is best left to pros with specialized know-how and equipment.

Made of acrylic and/or polyester, solid-surface material can be sawed, drilled, routed, sanded, and glued in much the same way as wood – but the dust and fumes from these operations are highly toxic and flammable.

Shop-built solid-surface counters needn't be run-of-the-mill, either. In fact, this versatile material lends itself to all sorts of design possibilities, such as inlays, specially routed edges, contrasting borders, and integral sinks.

Virtually invisible seams are made by filling the joint with solid-surface adhesive, then pulling it tight with specialized turnbuckles. Excess adhesive is later chiseled off and the surface is sanded smooth.

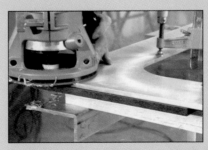

Borders are first shaped, then glued to the countertop. Here, the corner is rounded off with a router and a special jig. Later the border will be glued to the countertop.

Solid-surface backsplashes are joined to the countertop in the shop. Here the fabricator uses a router to shape a cove joint between the counter and the backsplash.

Cutting laminate

Cut the laminate ½ inch wider and longer than needed; you'll trim off the excess later.

The score and snap method is an easy way to cut laminate – all you need is a laminate scorer and a straightedge. If you choose to cut the laminate on a table saw, be sure to cut it face up; if you use a circular saw, support it on particleboard and cut it face down.

Laminating edges

The best place to laminate a countertop is a large, well-ventilated work area. To avoid getting debris in the contact cement, the work area should be as clean and dust-free as possible.

Begin by brushing contact cement on the edges of the substrate and the back sides of the laminate strips. Let the cement dry until it's tacky (about 10 minutes), then carefully position the laminate against the substrate. Go over the laminate with a J-roller, pressing hard to make a good bond.

Rout off the excess using a router with a flush-trimming bit. Then run a laminate file over the top edge to make sure the laminate is perfectly flush to the substrate. (The surfaces are flush if you feel no resistance to the file.)

1 *Score* the face of the laminate with a laminate scorer. Use a long straightedge or the edge of the substrate to guide the scorer. The laminate should overhang the substrate by ½ inch on all edges.

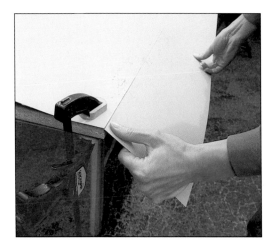

2 *Clamp* the scored laminate to a solid surface and snap it downward. The laminate should break cleanly along the score mark.

3 *Coat the laminate strips* and the substrate edges with contact cement. Most of the first coat will soak into the porous edge of the particleboard, so apply a second coat to the substrate after a few minutes. Let the cement dry until it's tacky.

4 *Align the edge strip* so it overhangs the top and bottom. Contact cement bonds instantly, so don't touch the strip to the particleboard until it's in position. Then, starting at one end, carefully press it onto the edge of the substrate.

5 *Remove* the overhang with a flush-cutting laminate router bit. Follow up with a laminate file to make sure the laminate and substrate are perfectly flush.

Laminating the top

The trick here is to keep the laminate and substrate apart until you've aligned the laminate. Thin strips of wood or cardboard, dowels, and slats salvaged from an old mini-blind all work well as spacers.

After the contact cement sets up, lay the spacers on the substrate and place the laminate, cement-side down, on top of the spacers. Align the laminate so it overlaps all edges, then, starting in the middle, pull out the spacers one by one, rolling the laminate as you go.

Use a router with a flush-cut bit to trim the excess. This leaves a very slight overhang, so finish up by using a laminate file held at a steep angle to take off the excess. Then shift to a 45-degree angle to create a slightly beveled edge.

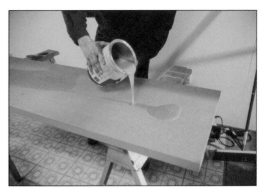

1 *Pour contact cement* straight from the can onto the substrate and the back side of the laminate. Work in a dust-free and well-ventilated room.

2 *Spread the contact cement* with a glue roller. Use a brush at the edges, taking care that you don't smear cement onto the edge strips.

3 *Lay spacer strips* across the substrate after the cement sets up, then position the laminate over the spacers. Align the laminate so it overlaps all edges.

4 *Starting in the middle,* remove the spacers one by one. Roll the laminate into the adhesive with a J-roller, but be careful around the edges – if you veer onto the overhang, you could crack the laminate.

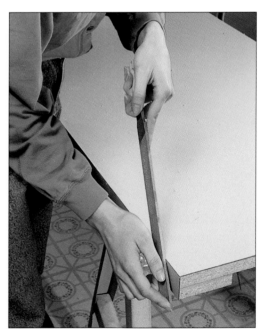

5 *To remove the slight overhang* left by the router, hold the laminate file at a steep angle and stroke downward until a bead of contact cement breaks away from the seam; then hold the file at 45 degrees and use long strokes to lightly bevel the edge.

Fabricating a backsplash

Cut a piece of particleboard to serve as a substrate for the backsplash. To create a scribe strip along the top edge and any exposed ends, glue and nail ¼-inch-thick strips of particleboard to the back of the substrate.

Apply laminate to the bottom of the backsplash, as well as to the face, top, and exposed edges. This way, when (not if) the caulked joint between the counter and backsplash fails, water won't seep in and warp the substrate before you get around to recaulking the joint. Laminate the edges before the face, so the seams will be less visible.

Scribing the backsplash

Set the backsplash in place and press it to the wall. Set a compass to the width of the widest gap and draw it along the length of the top edge. Use a belt sander to sand the scribe strip to the line. Check that the backsplash fits snug to the wall before installing it.

1 *Drive drywall screws* through each corner bracket up into the particleboard substrate to fasten the countertop to the cabinets. Make sure the screws are long enough to bore into the countertop, but not so long they go through the top.

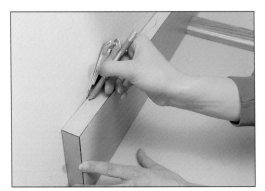

2 *To scribe a backsplash* to fit against an uneven wall, set a compass to the widest gap, hold the point against the wall, and pull the pencil along the top edge.

3 *Clamp the backsplash* to a workbench or other surface and sand the scribing strip down to the pencil line. Wear a mask, safety glasses, and hearing protection.

4 *Attach the backsplash* with silicone adhesive. The shims along the bottom edge bring it flush with what remains of the scribe strip.

5 *Press the backsplash* against the wall with clamps and strips of particleboard. To force it down against the counter, nail temporary cleats to the studs, then drive shims between the cleats and the top edge of the backsplash.

6 *Bore a starter hole,* then cut the sink opening with a jig saw (tape on the base plate keeps the saw from scratching the laminate). After cutting the sides, fasten scrap lumber to the cutout; this keeps the cutout from dropping out and chipping the laminate as you near the end of the cut.

Installing Sinks and Faucets

Spending time in the cramped quarters under a sink is no fun at all. Minimize your time down there by attaching the faucet and parts of the drain assembly to the sink before you set it in place.

Installing stop valves

To install stops, turn off the water at the meter, then cut off the caps you soldered to the stub-outs. Slip an escutcheon plate, a compression nut, and a compression ring onto each stub-out. Tightening the nut onto a stop valve squishes the ring for a watertight seal. Don't use pipe dope or Teflon tape with compression fittings.

Check for leaks

Before you turn the water on, unscrew the faucet's aerator so any debris in the line will be flushed away. Install the faucet handles, run the water full blast and, using a flashlight and your fingers, inspect each connection. If you find a leak, slightly tighten the connection.

1 *Fit the faucet valves* *and spout through holes in the sink deck and fasten them with locknuts. Coat threads with pipe dope or Teflon tape and run flex lines from the faucets to the spout.*

2 *Roll plumber's putty* *into a thick rope and wrap it around the threads on the flange. Press the flange into the drain opening.*

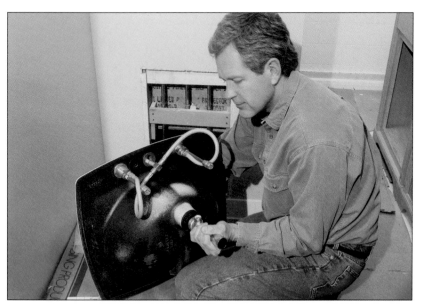

3 *Thread the tailpiece assembly* *onto the flange. Align the hole for the drain pop-up to the rear before tightening. Scrape away any putty that oozes from the flange.*

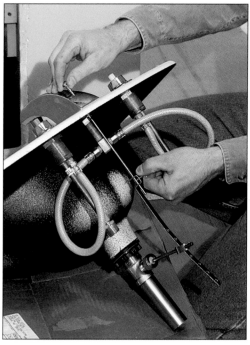

4 *Thread the pop-up* *assembly's lift rod into the tailpiece. Link the rod to the drain control and adjust the linkage so the drain opens and closes smoothly.*

Finally, close the stopper, fill the basin to the overflow, open the drain, and check the trap for leaks. Pressure from water in the sink will force water through any loose connection in the drain assembly.

6 *To install stop valves*, shut off the water, cut the caps from the supply pipes, and thread on new stops. Use two wrenches to tighten the compression fitting.

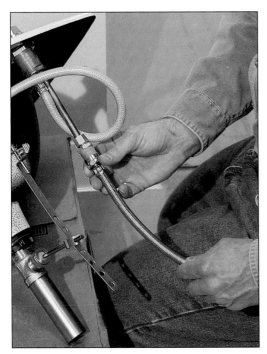

5 *Coat the threads* of the faucet supply lines with pipe dope or Teflon tape and screw on another set of flex lines. These will connect to the fixture stops.

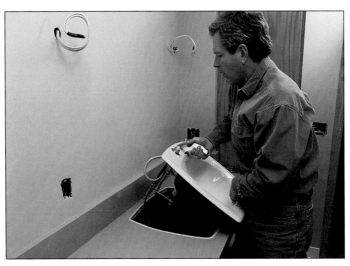

7 *Run two beads* of silicone adhesive around the edge of the sink cutout and set the sink in place. With some sinks you must also tighten brackets that clamp the sink to the underside of the counter.

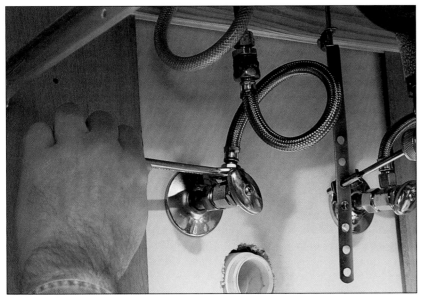

8 *Loop the flexible* supply lines, seal their threads with pipe dope or Teflon tape, and screw the lines to the stops. Don't turn on the water until you've installed the trap.

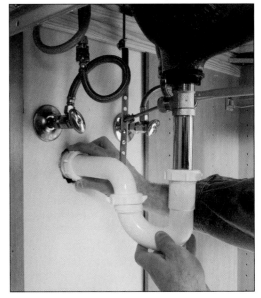

9 *Take apart the trap*, then slip the J-shaped piece onto the tailpiece and the L-shaped piece into the trap adapter. Align the pieces and tighten all the slip nuts.

Installing a cultured marble countertop

Installing a countertop with an integral sink is really pretty simple. First install the faucet and drain assemblies. Then, glue the countertop to the cabinets with silicone adhesive; usually it just takes a couple of dabs to hold the counter in place.

You can't scribe one of these to fit perfectly against the wall like you can with a laminate counter. Instead, just run a bead of caulk around the edges.

Installing a Toilet

If the old toilet didn't have a shut-off valve, install one now, before you bring in the new toilet. Otherwise, you'll be working in what is typically a very small space between the toilet and the stop.

Setting the bowl

Begin by laying the bowl upside down on part of the box it came in. Fit a wax ring with a plastic sleeve over the outlet, or horn.

Next, fit bolts into the floor flange. The bolts, called closet bolts, should be parallel with the wall behind the toilet. Slip the bowl over the closet bolts, then lean on the bowl to expand the wax ring for a tight seal.

The relationship of the water surface to the bowl is an important part of the design of a low-flush toilet. The bowl must be level or the flush action could be affected. It's also important that the bowl be stable. Rocking can break the drain seal and cause a leak. Use plastic shims to level and stabilize the bowl.

After you've leveled the bowl, hand thread nuts onto the closet bolts and tighten them with a nut driver. Tightening the nuts unevenly could throw the bowl off level, so continue to check level as you tighten the nuts.

1 **Turn the bowl upside down** and slip a wax ring with a sleeve onto the drain horn. The wax seals the drain to the floor flange.

2 **Slide closet bolts** into the floor flange. These may be provided by the manufacturer or you might need to buy them separately.

Setting the tank

Most toilets come with a turnkey tank; the supply and flush valves are already in place as are the gasket and hold-down bolts. If not, follow the manufacturer's directions for assembling the valves, spud washer, and bolts.

Align the tank's hold-down bolts with the holes in the bowl, and ease the tank into position. Thread nuts onto the bolts and tighten them, checking the tank for level side to side and front to back as you do. A level bowl and tank mean the hold-down bolts have been tightened evenly and are applying equal pressure across the gasket, and that the tank is now far less likely to leak where it meets the bowl.

Hooking up the supply line

Here you have two options: chrome tubing you cut and then bend to fit, or a flex line. Chrome tubing looks nice, but flex lines are easier to work with in tight spaces. Whichever you choose, coat all threads with pipe dope or Teflon tape before making connections.

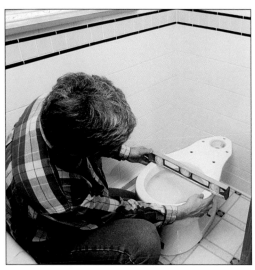

4 *Level the bowl* side to side and front to back. A low-flush toilet must have a level bowl to flush properly.

3 *Shut off the water*, uncap the stub-out, and fit it with a fixture stop. The stop's outlet should point upward. Don't overtighten it.

5 *To stabilize a bowl* that rocks, tip it very slightly and slip a plastic shim under the low side. Adjust the shim so the bowl is both level and stable.

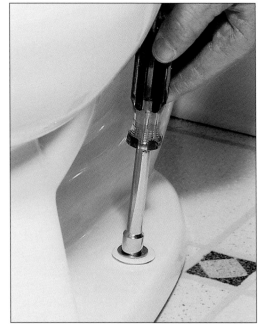

6 *Install washers* and hand tighten nuts onto the closet bolts. Check that the bowl is still level and go another half turn with a nut driver, taking care that you don't crack the china.

Handle with care

Toilets are far from delicate fixtures, but they're made of china, which can crack or even shatter if carelessly handled. Drop a piece or overtighten a bolt and you'll have to buy a whole new toilet.

7 *Align* the hold-down bolts with the holes in the bowl and set the tank in position on top of the bowl.

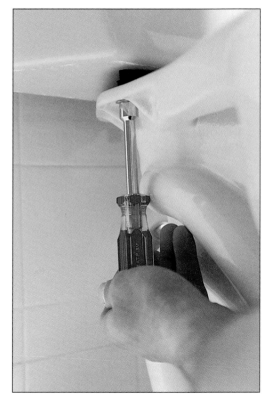

8 *Hand turn nuts* onto the tank bolts, then tighten them with a nut driver, checking that the tank is level side to side and front to back.

9 *Cut chrome tubing* (left) to length with a tubing cutter. Tubing has a threaded connection at the tank end and a compression fitting at the stop end. Flex line (right) comes in different lengths and has threaded fittings at both ends. It works better in tight spots like the one shown here. The tubing looks classier, but tends to kink when you try to bend it into sharp curves. If your shut-off is only a few inches from the tank inlet, use flex.

Final Trim-Outs

The hardest part of doing the final trim-outs is reading the directions. Most of the fixtures you install from this point on will come with assembly and installation instructions. Read them, follow them, and take your time so you don't damage the finish on the fittings and fixtures.

Protect chrome and enameled fittings against scratches. Wrap a rag or a piece of chamois around the fitting you're installing, or wrap tape around the pliers' jaws.

To install a showerhead, slip on an escutcheon plate, apply pipe dope or Teflon tape, hand tighten the head assembly, then go a final half turn or so with groove-joint pliers.

Spread cardboard on the new countertop before using it as a worktable. It protects the countertop and adds a little cushion in case you drop something breakable.

Make final electrical connections inside fixtures or junction boxes by connecting ground wires to ground, white wires to white, and black or red wires to black. Screw a wire connector onto each group of wires.

A cover plate or fixture base covers the wires on most fixtures; many also have a diffuser that shields the bulbs. Attach the cover plate, test the fixture, then install the diffuser.

Installing a shower door

Shower doors come in kits, and installation procedures vary. Begin any installation by reading the directions and laying out the parts to be sure nothing's missing.

Mark plumb layout lines for the track. To drill holes for the track anchors, use a ¼-inch bit. For ceramic tile walls, use a masonry bit. Tap wall anchors into the holes.

Hang the doors on the tracks, according to the manufacturer's directions.

Apply silicon caulk everywhere the tracks meet the walls and top of the tub, both inside and outside the tub.

Installing switches and receptacles

You can connect wires to switches and receptacles in one of two ways – by pushing them into holes in the back of the device, or by looping the wires around screws on one or both sides. The push-in terminals are a little faster and easier to use, but the screws provide a better grip, and it's easier to disconnect the wires later without damaging the device.

Whichever method you decide to use, shut off the power and remove about ¾ inch of insulation from the wires with a wire stripping tool. Then bend each wire into a loop that fits clockwise around a screw. (Wires that loop clockwise around the screw are pulled tight to the terminal as you tighten the screw.) Wires covered with white insulation go around silver terminals, attach black-insulated wires to brass terminals. Hook up ground, neutral, then hot wires.

Installing cabinet pulls

There's an easy way and a hard way to install cabinet hardware. The hard way involves measuring, marking, and drilling holes for each pull. This takes lots of time, and if you mess up, you end up with an ugly hole in the wrong place. It's quicker, easier, and (almost) goofproof to use a jig. Make one for the doors, another for the drawers.

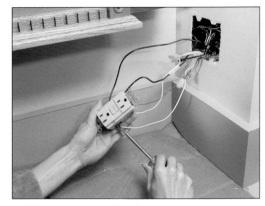

With GFCI receptacles, incoming power goes to the line terminals. Connect outgoing wires to lights or other receptacles to the load terminals.

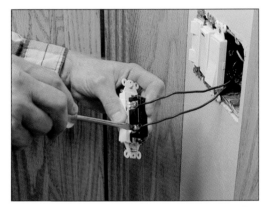

The switch controls current that flows through the black hot conductors from the power source, through the switch, and to the light. If the light is positioned between the power source and the switch, there may be one black and one white conductor (which could be hot) connected to the switch.

Speed up the installation of cabinet pulls with a jig. It locates holes right where you want them, time after time. You can make one from scrap lumber or buy one at a home center.

Restock the medicine cabinet, bring in some colorful towels and accessories – and enjoy the results. Within a couple of weeks you'll have forgotten all about the trials of remodeling and will think it was all well worth it.

Index